Places

PLACES

Identity, Image and Reputation

Simon Anholt

First published 2010 by
PALGRAVE MACMILLAN

Palgrave Macmillan in the UK is an imprint of Macmillan Publishers Limited, registered in England, company number 785998, of Houndmills, Basingstoke, Hampshire RG21 6XS.

Palgrave Macmillan in the US is a division of St Martin's Press LLC, 175 Fifth Avenue, New York, NY 10010.

Palgrave Macmillan is the global academic imprint of the above companies and has companies and representatives throughout the world.

Palgrave® and Macmillan® are registered trademarks in the United States, the United Kingdom, Europe and other countries

ISBN-13: 978-0-230-23977-7

This book is printed on paper suitable for recycling and made from fully managed and sustained forest sources. Logging, pulping and manufacturing processes are expected to conform to the environmental regulations of the country of origin.

A catalogue record for this book is available from the British Library.

A catalogue record for this book is available from the Library of Congress.

10 9 8 7 6 5 4 3 2
19 18 17 16 15 14 13 12 11 10

Printed and bound in Great Britain by
CPI Antony Rowe, Chippenham and Eastbourne

For Alexandra, Claudia and Luca

CONTENTS

List of Figure and Tables

Figure

Tables

Introduction

Let me be clear: there is no such thing as 'nation branding'. It is a myth, and perhaps a dangerous one.

In books and papers and lectures and talks over the last few years, I have repeated such sentiments so many times that somebody commented to me a while ago that I now spend more time explaining what I *don't* mean than what I *do* mean, and more time telling people what my subject is *not* about rather than what it *is* about.

This is disconcerting, but not surprising. In one sense I'm still paying the price of a careless piece of branding I did 14 years ago, when I coined the phrase *nation brand*. I little guessed how potent the combination of those two little words would prove to be, or what a double-edged sword the idea of branding would become when applied to countries, cities and regions.

On the one hand, 'brand' is a perfect metaphor for the way places compete with each other in the global marketplace for products, services, events, ideas, visitors, talent, investment and influence: this is simply the reality of globalization, and it's inescapable. On the other hand, 'branding' makes many people think of superficial marketing tricks, perhaps even some cynical betrayal of the nation state and other human communities. This is a misunderstanding, and an unfortunate one for many reasons.

These days I use the 'B-word' less and less, but it is still a useful metaphor and hard to dispense with altogether. It pops up fairly frequently in this book – partly because several of the essays I have included are my editorial prefaces from a journal I launched in 2004 and still edit, *Place Branding and Public Diplomacy*. I often refer to the international research programmes I have been conducting since 2005, the Anholt Nation Brands Index™ and Anholt City Brands Index™. I also quote from my previous books – *Brand New*

Justice and *Brand America* amongst others. So, try as I might, I cannot escape completely from the 'B-word', since it is attached to so much of my work. To some, it may seem perverse that I constantly try; but words are important, and it is problematic to have a word which many associate with superficiality and cynicism attached to a field of study and practice which, at least in my view, is most emphatically the opposite.

So, with apologies to regular readers of my work, I must once again preface this book with a brief summary of my basic position on the issue of places and their reputations.

Nations may have brands – in the sense that they have reputations, and those reputations are every bit as important to their progress and prosperity in the modern world as brand images are to corporations and their products – but the idea that it is possible to 'do branding' to a country (or to a city or region) in the same way that companies 'do branding' to their products, is both vain and foolish. In the 15 years since I first started working in this field I have not seen a shred of evidence, a single properly researched case study, to show that marketing communications programmes, slogans or logos, have ever succeeded, or could ever succeed, in directly altering international perceptions of places.

In fact there is some evidence to suggest the opposite: between 2005 when the Anholt Nation Brands Index[1] was launched, and the latest study in 2009, there has been no detectable correlation between changes in national image and expenditure on 'nation branding campaigns'. Several countries which have done no marketing (aside from normal tourism and investment promotion) during this period have shown noticeable improvements in their overall images, while others have spent extremely large sums on advertising and PR campaigns and their brand value has remained stable or even declined.

I continually repeat this mantra partly because I long to be contradicted. It would be fascinating to see some evidence that international perceptions of countries really can be influenced by marketing communications techniques, and such proof would have important, far-reaching and frankly rather alarming consequences. Yet I have seen no such evidence, nor even heard any very convincing arguments in favour of it: I see a good deal of research showing that *tourism* campaigns can persuade people to go on holiday to a certain country, but there's nothing surprising or controversial about that – everybody knows that products or services can be effectively sold to a target audience using marketing communications. And I occasionally see research showing that 'nation-branding' campaigns are effective in so far as they succeed in creating awareness and even recall amongst certain target audiences, but there's nothing surprising about that either. If you repeat a slogan frequently enough, people will end up recognizing it, and may even be able to repeat it when asked. Whether it actually has the power to alter their opinions and their behaviour towards that country is quite another matter.

Yet all around the world, in country after country and city after city, such marketing campaigns are cheerfully sold to governments, and billions of dollars of public money are spent producing them and placing them in the media, where they disappear without a trace.

In truth, nation branding is the problem, not the solution. It is public opinion which brands countries – in other words, reduces them to the weak, simplistic, outdated, unfair stereotypes that so damage their prospects in a globalized world – and most countries need to *fight against* the tendency of international public opinion to brand them, not encourage it. Governments need to help the world understand the real, complex, rich, diverse nature of their people and landscapes, their history and heritage, their products and their resources: to *prevent* them from becoming mere brands.

Since I first used the phrase 'nation brand' in 1996, the idea has created some excitement in government circles in many countries, thanks to the tantalizing but illusory prospect of a quick fix for a weak or negative national image. The combination of the words 'nation' and 'brand' has so much resonance partly because there is an important truth here: the brand *images* of places are indeed central to their progress and prosperity. This was my point. Today, the world is one market; the advance of globalization means that every country, city and region must compete with every other for its share of the world's commercial, political, social and cultural transactions. In such an environment, as in any busy marketplace, brand image becomes a critical factor; the necessary short cut to an informed buying decision.

The effect of national brand image is plain to see. Countries, cities and regions that are lucky or virtuous enough to have acquired a positive reputation find that everything they or their citizens wish to do on the global stage is easier: their brand goes before them, opening doors, creating trust and respect, and raising the expectation of quality, competence and integrity.

Places with a reputation for being poor, uncultured, backward, dangerous or corrupt find that everything they or their citizens try to achieve outside their own neighbourhood is harder, and the burden is always on their side to prove that they don't conform to the national stereotype. Compare the experiences of a Swedish and an Iranian manager on the international job market, or the struggles of an exporter from Bangladesh with one from Canada. Compare the ease with which a mediocre tourist resort in a highly regarded country can gain glowing media coverage and celebrity endorsement, with the difficulties experienced by an unspoiled and unique destination in a country with a weak or poor reputation. Compare the way consumers in Europe or America will willingly pay more for an unknown 'Japanese' product than for an identical 'Korean' product that is probably made in the same Chinese factory. Compare how positively the international media will report on an ordinary piece of policy from the government of a country reputed to be fair, rich and stable, with the media silence or sharp criticism which greets a wise, brave and innovative policy from a country that's saddled with a negative image.

In short, nobody doubts that places have their brand images, and that those images are critical to their success in the many international contests that characterize the modern economy. It's only when people start talking about *branding* rather than just *brand* that the problems start.

It would certainly make life easier for many governments if it were possible to brand places: it would conveniently reduce the success criteria for their economic and political competitiveness to having a big enough marketing budget and hiring the best marketing and PR agencies. But of course the reality is more complex; national images are not created through communications, and cannot be altered by communications.

One might well ask, if marketing communications work so well for products and services, why shouldn't they work for countries and cities?

One simple answer is that they *don't* work so well for products and services – or at least, not in the way that most casual observers suppose. Although great advertising, attractive logos and memorable slogans are strongly associated with powerful commercial brands, they aren't the reason why those brands are powerful: brands become powerful when the product behind them earns trust. This happens as a consequence of many *sales*, leading to many direct customer experiences, and a product that fulfils or exceeds its promise. The advertising campaigns generate the sales; they only build the brand indirectly.

Because countries and cities aren't for sale, the marketing communications campaigns associated with them can only be empty propaganda: instead of saying 'please try this product' they are only saying 'please change your mind about this country', and the message misfires.

Brand management in the commercial sphere only works because the company that owns the brand has a high degree of control over the product itself and over its channels of communication, and so can directly influence both consumers' experience of the product, and the way in which the product is presented to them through the media. A good company with a good product can, with sufficient skill, patience and resources, build the brand image it wants and needs and which its product deserves – but no more than its product deserves.

Places are utterly different. No single body, political or otherwise, exercises nearly this much control either over the national 'product' or the way it communicates with the outside world. The tiniest village is infinitely more complex, more diverse and less unified than the largest corporation, because of the different reasons why people are there. Places have no single, unifying purpose, unlike the simple creed of shareholder value that binds corporations together: a contract of employment is mainly about duties, whereas a social contract is mainly about rights. Of course, there have always been heads of state who attempt to run their countries like corporations and exercise control over the 'brand' by controlling the channels of information, but this kind of control through propaganda can only work within entirely closed societies. It is one of the positive side-effects of globalization that in our media-literate and constantly communicating international arena, propaganda is not so much evil as impossible.

Another reason why national or city images can't be changed so easily is because they are so robust. National image, as the Nation Brands Index shows, is a remarkably stable phenomenon, more a fixed asset than a liquid currency. We all seem to need these comforting stereotypes that enable us to put countries and cities in convenient pigeon-holes, and will only abandon them if we really have no other choice. The relevance of foreign places to most people is limited, and if, for example, a person in Germany or South Africa or Indonesia only spends a few moments each year thinking about Holland, it's not surprising if their perception of Holland remains largely unchanged for years on end. Images of foreign countries are truly part of the culture of the country which holds the perceptions: Holland's image in Germany is part of the German culture, and vice versa.

National reputation cannot be constructed; it can only be earned; and imagining that such a deeply rooted phenomenon can be shifted by so weak an instrument as marketing communications is an extravagant delusion. I am fond of quoting Socrates on this point: 'the way to achieve a better reputation is to endeavour to *be* what you desire to appear.'

Whilst governments cannot hope to manipulate the perceptions of millions of people in other countries, there are three important things that they *can* do about their national reputation:

- First, they can understand and monitor their international image, in the countries and sectors where it matters most to them, in a rigorous and scientific way, and understand exactly how and where this affects their interests in those countries and sectors,

- Second, if they collaborate imaginatively, effectively and openly with business and civil society, governments can agree on a national strategy and narrative – the 'story' of who the nation is, where it is going and how it is going to get there – which honestly reflects the skills, the genius and the will of the people.
- Third, governments can ensure that their country maintains a stream of innovative and eye-catching products, services, policies and initiatives in every sector, which keeps it at the forefront of the world's attention and admiration; demonstrates the truth of that narrative; and *proves* the country's right to the reputation its people and government desire to acquire.

More engagement, not simply more communication, with the rest of the world can enhance the profile of places, and higher visibility does tend to go together with stronger appeal.

The idea of national reputation isn't important simply because people find it intellectually appealing. For the majority of nations, the need to study, to understand, and to think about ways of influencing their international reputation is no longer really a matter of choice: either one takes some control over one's national reputation or one allows it to be controlled by public opinion and public ignorance. The catastrophic consequences of the latter are understood all too well by most African nations.

Not every government, and indeed not every population, treats international approval as an important goal, but when we speak of the brand images of places, we are talking about something rather more significant than mere popularity.

The only sort of government that can afford to ignore the impact of its national reputation is one which has no interest in participating in the global community, and no desire for its economy, its culture or its citizens to benefit from the rich influences and opportunities that the rest of the world offers them.

It is the duty of every responsible government in the age of globalization to recognize that the nation's reputation, one of the most valuable assets of its people, is given to it in trust for the duration of its office. Its duty is to hand that reputation down to its successors, whatever their political persuasion, in at least as good health as it received it, and to improve it if possible for the benefit of future generations.

There seems little doubt that if the world's governments placed even half the value that most wise corporations have learned to place on their good names, the world would be a safer and quieter place than it is today.

This is why the subject of places and their identities, their reputations and their images, is such a rich and rewarding topic. But we can only access the real importance and the real fascination of the topic if we abandon the notion that 'place branding' – or, as I prefer to call it, competitive identity – is some form of marketing discipline.

It is nothing less than a new approach to statecraft, to economic development and international relations. I have chosen the essays in this collection to try and sketch out some of the outer boundaries of this exhilarating new subject.

CHAPTER 1

Images of Place: Is This About Marketing, or Isn't It?

As one ploughs through the ever-increasing quantity of blogs, articles, interviews and academic papers where place 'branding' or public diplomacy are discussed – and interestingly enough, more and more of them mention both ideas in the same context – I get a sense that one important message may finally be starting to permeate the community of academics and practitioners: that communications are no substitute for policies, and that altering the image of a country or city may require something a little more substantial than graphic design, advertising or PR campaigns.

Certainly, I still hear with depressing regularity of national, regional and city governments putting out tenders for 'branding agencies', and funding lavish marketing campaigns of one sort or another, all in an effort to enhance their national or international images. Still, a rising number of commentators have taken on board the idea that it is principally deeds which create public perceptions, not words and pictures. 'It's not about logos and slogans' (or, at any rate, 'it's not *just* about logos and slogans') is a mantra that has become almost universal, now dutifully repeated even by the consulting firms whose commercial lifeblood is the purveying of logos and slogans. Presumably they hope thereby to sell even more profitable strategic advice alongside the graphic design and advertising copy.

Perhaps good sense is at last beginning to prevail; perhaps some policy makers have started to ask themselves when was the last time *they* changed their minds about something they had believed for most of their lives just because an advertisement told them to. Perhaps those same policy makers, seized with an unprecedented academic rigour and a new desire to make their public expenditures accountable and measurable, have even started to search around for properly documented case studies to prove how marketing campaigns have demonstrably and measurably improved the international image of nations, and have failed to find a single one.

More research is needed in this area, and a clearer distinction between selling campaigns such as tourism and investment promotion – which may well improve sales within their specific sectors and among their specific audiences but may have little or no effect on the overall image of the country – and so-called nation branding campaigns. Establishing clarity on this point is difficult because remarkably few nation branding initiatives appear to include any provision for measuring their impact or effectiveness. Considering that it is usually taxpayers' or donors' money being spent on such campaigns, this is surprising.

The view that actions speak louder than words is quite commonly heard in discussions of public diplomacy (one felicitous phrase used in this context was 'the diplomacy of deeds', coined by Karen Hughes, until 2008 the US State Department's Under-Secretary for Public Diplomacy). The state of the debate in place branding circles lags far behind, however, and formulations such as 'nation branding is the application of consumer marketing techniques to countries in order to improve their image' are, alas, the rule rather than the exception, and are still used in the majority of the academic and practitioner papers submitted to the journal which I edit, *Place Branding and Public Diplomacy.*

This difference in attitudes between the two fields may be because commentators in public diplomacy more often come from a background of foreign affairs or international relations than marketing, and are consequently more used to dealing with reality than perception. It may also be because the field of public diplomacy predates the field of place branding by some 40 or 50 years, so it is not surprising if the prevailing view is a more mature one.

Those commentators who espouse the 'actions not words' school of thought, as I do, may feel, like me, as if they expend more time and energy explaining what public diplomacy and place branding *aren't* than what they are, and in discussions about place branding they can appear to be in the grip of a permanent identity crisis: they inhabit a field with a name that clearly doesn't quite suit it. The branding, in other words, is all wrong.

The appropriateness of the word 'brand' to describe an approach which I, at any rate, prefer to call *competitive identity,* is certainly a vexed question. Once people actually receive the message that this thing called 'branding' is not about communications but about policy change, many will ask the following legitimate and per-tinent questions – and if they ask me, will receive the following answers:

Q: *So if place branding is not about communications but policies, why is it branding?*

A: It *isn't* branding. One starts with the observation that places have images just as products and corporations have images, and that places depend to a similar extent on the power and appeal of those images for their progress and prosperity. But there is a big dif-ference between observing that places *have brand images* (which is just a useful metaphor) and claiming that places *can be branded* (which is an excessively ambitious, entirely unproven and ultimately irresponsible claim). Place branding, as I originally intended the term to be understood, observes the former but does not claim the latter. There are certainly policy approaches which enable places to improve the speed, efficiency and effectiveness with which they achieve a better image – or else I would be out of a job – but that better image can only be earned; it cannot be constructed or invented.

Q: *So if place branding is not about communications but policies, what gives branding people the right or the ability to advise in this area?*

A: It gives them no right to do so, and indeed relatively little prep-aration. A branding expert will need to become a policy expert in order to advise on policy, just as a farmer will need to become a software expert in order to advise on software; but it is possible that their previous expertise may bring some extra dimension to the advice they give. There is nothing to stop people retraining and then purveying advice in their new field, and their clients will decide for themselves whether their advice is worth paying for; but relatively little of what one might learn as a branding or marketing expert is truly transferable or useful in the fields of policy-making, international relations, public diplomacy, cultural relations and the other components of competitive identity.

Q: *So if place branding is not about communications but policies, what's new about it, and why bother to give it a new name?*
A: There are, in essence, five new ideas within place branding or competitive identity:

1. Places must engage with the outside world in a clear, coordinated and communicative way if they are to influence public opinion. A robust and productive coalition between government, business and civil society, as well as the creation of new institutions and structures to achieve and maintain this behaviour, is necessary for achieving this harmonization of goals, themes, communications and behaviours in the long term.
2. The notion of *brand image* is critical: reputation understood as an external, even cultural phenomenon which is not under the direct control of the 'owner' of the brand but which nonetheless is a critical factor that underpins every transaction between the brand and its consumers.
3. The notion of *brand equity* is critical: the idea that reputation is a hugely valuable asset that needs to be managed, measured, protected, leveraged and nurtured over the long term.
4. The notion of *brand purpose* is critical: the idea that uniting groups of people around a common strategic vision can create a powerful dynamic for progress, and that brand management is first and foremost an *internal* project.
5. The importance of sustained and coherent *innovation* in all sectors of national activity if public opinion is to be influenced: international public opinion, and in consequence the media, is far more interested in new things that suggest a clear and attractive pattern of development and ability within the country or city, than in the rehearsal of past glories.

If these five concepts are understood and responsibly applied by policy makers, they can bring a powerful new dimension to development, statecraft and governance. Together, they represent a genuinely new approach to the way in which places need to be managed in the age of globalization, and the coining of a new term to describe this approach appears justified.

Q: *So if place branding is not about communications but policies, why do so many countries with good policies still suffer from a weak or negative reputation?*
A: Because policies alone, even if effectively implemented, are not sufficient to persuade foreign publics to part with their existing pre-judices and perceptions, which in the case of national images may prove exceptionally resilient to change. **Substance** must be coupled with **strategy** and frequent **symbolic actions** if it is to result in an enhanced reputation.

Strategy, in its simplest terms, is knowing *who* a nation is and *where* it stands today (both in reality and according to internal and external perceptions); knowing where it wants to get to; and knowing how it is going to get there. The two main difficulties associated with strategy development are (a) reconciling the needs and desires of a wide range of different national actors into a more or less single direction, and (b) finding a strategic goal that is both inspiring and feasible, since these two requirements are frequently contradictory.

Substance is the effective execution of that strategy in the form of new economic, legal, political, social, cultural and educational activity: the real innovations, structures, legislation, reforms, investments, institutions and policies which will bring about the desired progress.

Symbolic actions are a particular species of substance that happen to have an intrinsic communicative power: they might be innovations, structures, legislation, reforms, investments, institutions or policies which are especially suggestive, remarkable, memorable, picturesque, newsworthy, topical, poetic, touching, surprising or dramatic. Most importantly, they are emblematic of the strategy: they are at the same time a component of the national story and the means of telling it.

Some good examples of symbolic actions are the Slovenian government donating financial aid to their Balkan neighbours in order to prove that Slovenia wasn't part of the Balkans; Spain legalizing single-sex marriages in order to demonstrate that its values had modernized to a point diametrically opposed to the Franco period; the decision of the Irish government to exempt artists, writers and poets from income tax in order to prove the state's respect for creative talent; Estonia declaring internet access to be a human right; or the Hague hosting the European Court of Human Rights (partly) in order to cement the Netherlands' reputation as a global bastion of the rule of law.

A building, such as the Guggenheim Museum in Bilbao or the Sydney Opera House, may have a symbolic value for its city and country well beyond its economic 'footprint'; and places with no chance of being selected to host major sporting or cultural events are often observed to bid for them, apparently just in order to communicate the fact that they are internationally engaged, ambitious, and proud of their achievements. Even simple publicity stunts, such as 'The Best Job in the World', Tourism Queensland's international recruitment drive for an 'islands caretaker' in early 2009, can become symbolic acts that – in return for a remarkably small investment – create widespread 'viral' interest in places.

Often the symbolic power of such an action can't be predicted, as its full effect derives from an imponderable fusion of the action itself, the moment and context in which it appears, the mood and culture of the 'audience', and their perceptions of the place where it originates. The 'Best Job in the World', by accident or by design, sat neatly at the intersection between a number of powerful ideas: the existing, positive 'brand' of Australia; the popularity of one kind of reality show that puts young adults into challenging environments and another kind where they compete for a dream job; the collapse of international financial markets and a consequent surge of interest in escape from modern urban reality; concern about climate change and the protection of vulnerable environments, especially coral reefs; and much else besides.

Such actions can also be planned; but the three most important points are:

1. A single symbolic action will seldom achieve any lasting effect: multiple actions should emanate from as many different sectors

as possible in order to build a rounded and believable image for the place.

2. They should never be *empty* – they must be communicative substance rather than just communication. Each symbolic action must be intrinsically defensible against the accusation of empty rhetoric, even when taken out of context and scrutinized on its own account (as commentators in a healthy democracy are bound to do).

3. They should continue in an unbroken succession for many years. Building a reputation in our busy modern world is like trying to fill a bathtub with the plug pulled out: as soon as each symbolic action is completed, its effect on public attention begins to decay, and unless it is swiftly followed by further and equally remarkable *proof* of the kind of country that produces it, that country's reputation will stand still or move backwards, and the bathtub will never fill.

It is clear that places require new and dedicated structures to coordinate, conceive, develop, maintain and promote such an unbroken chain of proof. None of the traditional apparatus of trade or government is fit for such a purpose – at least not in a way that cuts across all areas of national activity and is capable of sustaining it for the years and decades it takes to enhance, refine or otherwise alter the international image of a nation.

The concept of strategy plus substance plus symbolic actions is a classic 'three-legged stool': an approach that cannot stand up unless all three conditions are met.

Strategy + Substance – Symbolic Actions = Anonymity

Countries, for example, that succeed in developing a *strategy* and are diligent at creating real *substance* on the basis of this strategy but overlook the importance of *symbolic actions* still run the risk of remaining anonymous, undervalued, or unable to change the long-standing clichés of their international reputation, because strategies are often private and substance is often boring. Without the communicative power of symbolic actions, such countries can remain trapped inside a weak, distorted or outdated brand image for generations, and consequently fail to attract the consumers, talent, media attention, tourists and investors they need in order to build their economies, expand their influence and achieve their aims.

> *Substance – Strategy + Symbolic Actions = Incoherence*

Substance without an underlying *strategy* may achieve sporadic and localized economic and social benefits, but it is unlikely to build the country's profile or influence in any substantial way. Even if the substance is accompanied by frequent *symbolic actions*, without an underlying strategic intent the messages will remain fragmented, and no compelling or useful story of the nation's progress will form in the public consciousness.

> *Strategy – Substance – Symbolic Actions = Spin*

Strategy without *substance* is spin: it is the frequent predicament of weak governments that they make many plans but lack the willpower, the resources, the influence, the expertise or the public support to carry them to fruition.

> *Strategy – Substance + Symbolic Actions = Propaganda*

Strategy that is accompanied by *symbolic actions* but no real *substance* is worse still: this is authentic propaganda, a deliberate and schemed manipulation of public opinion designed to make people believe something different from reality. In today's world, where the globalization of communications has resulted in an environment where no single message can survive unchallenged, propaganda has become virtually impossible, and such an approach will result in the destruction of the country's good name for generations.

> *Symbolic Actions – Substance – Strategy = Failure*

Governments that focus purely on *symbolic actions* and fail to provide either *strategy* or real *substance* will soon be recognized as lightweights: carried this way and that by public opinion, and intent purely on achieving popularity, they seldom remain in power for long.

Clearly, the deliberate and planned use of symbolic actions can lay governments open to the charge of 'playing to the gallery', and devising strategies purely or largely in virtue of their impact on national image. Such behaviour, it could be argued, is even worse than simple propaganda, as it commits more public resources to the task of creating a certain impression than mere messages do. Each case must be judged on its own merits, but it could be argued that a symbolic action can be defended against the charge of propaganda if it is based on a clear long-term *strategy* and is supported by a substantially larger investment in real *substance.*

In the end, it is largely a matter of quantity that determines such a judgment: if nine out of ten policies or investments are selected purely on the basis that they benefit the country, and one on the basis that it gets the story across too, governments may act not only with a clear conscience, but also in the knowledge that the 10% of symbolic actions, by enhancing the reputation of the country, are adding substantial value to the other investments and thus may ultimately contribute even more value to the country than its more weighty but less media-friendly initiatives.

What governments sometimes have difficulty understanding is that the size, ambition or cost of initiatives may not be proportional to their symbolic value. Very large buildings which simply communicate wealth and hubris may have less power over the popular imagination than very small ones which happen to tell a story (in the City Brands Index, the tiny statue of the *mannekin pis* in Brussels is spontaneously mentioned by 20 times more international respondents than the enormous atomium, or even the gigantic headquarters of the European Commission; the government of Slovenia donating a few hundreds of thousands of Euros to Albania, Montenegro and Macedonia is more newsworthy than the US government donating hundreds of millions of dollars to Africa; one patient deprived of a hospital bed briefly generated more media coverage in the UK than the Labour government's injection of many billions of pounds into the National Health Service).

The substantial, strategically-informed symbolic actions which help to move national images forwards are not to be confused with the symbolic gestures that punctuate the history books – gestures which really have little substance in themselves but are sufficiently symbolic (in other words, media-friendly) to have real impact, memorability, popular appeal, and hence the power to change opinion and even behaviours: British Prime Minister Neville Chamberlain waving his truce with Hitler, Mahatma Gandhi sitting cross-legged at his weaving loom, Japanese Prime Minister Junichiro Koizumi visiting the Yasukuni shrine, the removal of Stalin's body from the Lenin Mausoleum in Moscow's Red Square in 1961, Sir Walter Raleigh laying his cloak over a puddle so that Queen Elizabeth I could keep her shoes dry, or Jesus Christ washing the feet of his disciples. And in fact there are plenty of examples of equally effective symbols which aren't gestures but words: Bismarck's 'blood and iron', Churchill's 'never before in the field of human conflict', Martin Luther King's 'I have a dream', and so forth.

Although these gestures and words are, in their own way, powerful 'brands', they are in a different category from the symbolic actions described earlier. Some of them only acquire their symbolic power much later through the retelling and the understanding that they crystallized an important turning-point in history; all of them owe most of their power to the highly significant or critical circumstances in which they occur. In other words, they are good rhetoric, whether this is deliberate or accidental.

Almost any word or gesture can become significant if it is delivered by an important person in a moment of crisis, and this is an important distinction to make when we are speaking of competitive identity, because the task in hand is usually quite different: the challenge in competitive identity is often to attract the attention of an indifferent public, to create a sense of momentousness when in fact most people are convinced that nothing of interest is going on.

This brings us right back to the original debate about whether national image really does have anything to do with branding, or whether the word is being used in a purely metaphorical sense. For this challenge is unquestionably the same one which gives rise to the discipline of marketing in the first place: it's the art or science of thrusting something into people's attention when people don't believe that it deserves to be there.

Whether they like it or not, countries and cities and regions in the age of global competition all need to market themselves: the most effective methods for doing this may owe little to the art of selling consumer goods, yet the challenge is precisely the same.

But then, didn't the wisest marketers always know that the most important aspect of any marketing initiative was the quality of the product? Good advertising, as Bill Bernbach once remarked, can only make a bad product fail faster: and the same is most certainly true of places.

CHAPTER 2

On Image and Trust

Notwithstanding my misgivings about the word, it's remarkable how widespread the concept of 'brand' has become in recent years: national, regional and city development certainly isn't the only non-commercial area where the word gets used more and more frequently.

It's obvious why this is so. 'Brand' is a word that captures the idea of reputation observed, reputation valued and reputation managed; and we live in a world in which reputation counts for a great deal. The importance of reputation, in fact, tends to increase as societies become larger, more diffuse and more complex: this is because most human transactions depend on trust in order to proceed.

Trust can either be formed through direct experience of the 'offering' by the 'purchaser' – what might be called *earned trust* – or else vicariously, following the example of other purchasers who have learned to trust the offering through their own direct experience. Trust formed in others is then used as a proxy for earned trust: this effect might be called *trust taken on trust*.

Trust formed by many satisfied purchasers creates a 'cloud' of trustworthiness which, perhaps quite naturally or perhaps with a little help, eventually surrounds an offering in the marketplace, and this cloud is a fundamental characteristic of strong brands. It performs the vital function of bridging the trust gap faced by first-time purchasers until they too have direct experience of the offering.

Of course, the appeal of the offering itself can also help to bridge this trust gap: when an offering is sufficiently desirable, purchasers will sometimes overlook their lack of direct experience of it, or even, on occasion, the absence of that cloud of trust which comes from the experiences of others. They will, in short, choose to trust their feelings rather than their reason.

The appeal of an offering, especially if combined with a cloud of trust, can sometimes be so powerful that it will even survive a negative direct experience. Appeal is largely subjective, and can be judged at surface by the purchasers, but quality, dependability, reliability, competence and trustworthiness are hidden from the eye and can only be learned by direct or indirect experience. Appeal can have its own cloud effect too, which is important for those purchasers who are unable or unwilling to form or rely on their own judgments about the appeal of the offering.

The cloud of trust and the cloud of appeal are fundamental to the success of most offerings in most marketplaces. The art and science of branding, design, advertising, public relations and public affairs are essentially processes by which this cloud of trust can be enhanced and its formation accelerated, even artificially induced or simulated. Companies and governments spend uncounted millions in attempting to create the impression that they are trusted by many people, or at least that they deserve this trust.

Globalization has created a vast, planet-sized network of individuals working, communicating and trading together, and in such a colony only a small proportion of transactions are able to proceed on a rational basis of earned trust. Human society therefore utterly depends on a vast and complex system of brand value in order to operate at this scale – a system entirely predicated on 'trust taken on trust'.

This system of trust clouds has taken several centuries to achieve its current state of development. In *Brand New Justice,* I argued that modern branding started in early fourteenth-century Italy, when certain family names emerged as symbols of wealth, trust and integrity: the Buonsignori of Siena – the first major international bank – then the Frescobaldi of Florence, the Ricciardi of Lucca, and later still, the Bardi, Peruzzi and Acciaiuoli families, some of whose business empires employed hundreds of staff in subsidiary offices across Europe and the Middle East and North Africa.[2]

In their correspondence and journals, the medieval Italian merchants stress over and over again the importance of creating a good and famous name: to be recognized far and wide as honourable citizens, to play a distinguished part in social and civic life, to support culture and donate to good causes. It is most interesting how this aspect of corporate reputation, never forgotten or overlooked by most clever and successful companies, has recaptured the attention of big business in recent decades, and the idea has been relaunched and rebranded as 'corporate social responsibility' or 'corporate citizenship', as if it were something that had just been invented.

Only an impeccable reputation for probity, substantial resources and success could automatically confer the kind of trust among new clients which ensured the continuation of their business. In every respect, the power of these family names was identical to that of modern brands: they acted as a shortcut to an informed buying or investing decision, and stood as a universally-acknowledged proxy for trust.

Ever since the publication of what was probably the first ever international business best-seller, the snappily-titled *Book of Knowledge of the Beauties of Commerce and of Cognisance of Good and Bad Merchandise and of Falsifications,* written by Abu al-Fadl Ja'far Ibn Ali of Damascus some time between the ninth and twelfth centuries, it has been understood that one's good name is worth more than riches, for the simple reason that it is the necessary basis for continued enrichment. People will only buy from people whom they know and trust, but as soon as trade extends beyond the limits of close acquaintances – which of course it must, if larger fortunes are to be made – then one's good name must somehow be broadcast, and become a byword for trustworthiness. The cloud of trust, in other words, must be created.

In exactly the same way as non-locally-produced products need brand names based on a reputation for quality in order to stand in for personal experience, so trading families – the service brands of their day – needed brand names based on a reputation for honour as soon as their circle of trade extended beyond the home town or a day's ride on horseback. Brands are a necessary consequence of the growing distance between buyer and seller; and this distance is a necessary function of the desire to expand the business to benefit from a wider marketplace.

Fast forward to today, and our globalized world is a world made almost entirely of brand value: we hardly ever do business with people we really know, and consequently live, work, and trade almost exclusively among clouds of trust. When the system is operating well, the benefits of trust tend to spread, but equally, a failure of trust also tends to spread, and can ultimately cause the entire system to collapse. The present global recession is a perfect illustration of a collapsing trust system. Many would say that the force of gravity is an intrinsic hazard of living in the clouds.

The trust broadcast system commonly called branding is most often associated with commercial transactions, simply because branding is a science that has developed within the commercial world, but the same basic principles apply in equal measure to almost every sphere of public and private life: political, social, and cultural, official and unofficial, private and public. The idea of place branding is usually associated with places simply because the nation, city or region is most often the administrative unit under whose authority the groups of people represented can behave in the organized manner necessary to achieve a 'branding' effect; but you can take the place away from place branding and the concept still stands.

Groups of people are subject to the branding effect just as places are: they are perceived both internally and externally as summarizable entities, and thus have 'brand images'; their wellbeing and prosperity are to a large extent conditioned and influenced by that image. So non-geographical groups of people are just as much 'nation brands' as places are: being a member of a particular faith, a caste, a social class or an income bracket, a political persuasion, an age group, a gang, a supporters' club, a profession, a gender: all these allegiances consign their individual members to a group branding effect, a public identity which overlays, influences and to some extent distorts their individual identity. Just as with a corporation or a country, the brand image of the group to which one is perceived to belong will help one to 'trade at a premium' if it is a positive image, and oblige one to 'trade at a discount' if it is negative. Weak or small groups, just like weak or small nations, can punch above their weight if their image magnifies the reality; and vice versa.

One is unavoidably 'branded' by one's social standing, income group, regional identity and educational level, and this too has a profound effect on one's prospects. In *The Spirit Level*,[3] Richard Wilkinson and Kate Pickett show that it is inequality, rather than poverty, that causes higher rates of crime, unemployment, unhappiness, physiological and mental illness, illiteracy and almost every conceivable social ill; and that many of these effects spread right through unequal societies, rather than being restricted to those at the bottom of the heap. Societies, in other words, have a habit of 'branding' their different strata and the individuals within them; and the fact itself of forever bearing and wearing that brand, like a uniform one can't take off, creates profound and far-reaching psychological effects.

In an unequal society, claim Wilkinson and Pickett, having visible inequality constantly paraded in front of one's eyes leads to stress and alienation, and ultimately to ill-health and crime. If this is the case within societies, why not also between societies? After all, one of the notable features of the globalization of the media is that images of extreme prosperity are now beamed into the poorest corners of the planet: could it be that globalization is simply serving to magnify and broadcast the negative effects of *planetary* inequality, and thus creating a global upsurge in the kinds of social evils that Wilkinson and Pickett describe at a national level?

Just to pick one of the many examples cited in the book of stress created by the awareness of inequality, a phenomenon known as 'stereotype threat' causes members of ethnic groups that are perceived as inferior to perform worse in academic tests when they are told that their abilities are being judged alongside members of higher-status groups. If such an effect operates on African-American students in US schools, what if it operated at a greatly magnified meta-level in that most unequal of societies, the planet? What if exporters from Sierra Leone or Rwanda, attempting to develop and market products in the global marketplace, felt similarly constrained by the knowledge that they were competing directly against producers in higher-status countries? Might this not depress their performance in just the same way? And supposing the effects of global inequality don't merely suppress performance, but as in the national cases, they also generate a vast range of social problems? Magnifying this effect on a planetary scale is a truly terrifying prospect.

To return to the smaller-scale 'branding' of sub-national groups, it should be stressed that borders and cultures don't always align, and the country and the nation are by no means always synonymous. Catalans live in a country called Spain, but for many, their identity is Catalonian before it is Spanish; the 'brand image' of Spain in the international popular imagination contains some elements that reflect their true identity, and others that don't. Perceptions, in other words, put them in the wrong box, and this creates discomfort. Any ethnic or linguistic minority which is 'branded' as part of a country that it sees as foreign or oppressive, at the expense of what it regards as its true identity, greatly compounds the sense of injustice created by the more material problems of inadequate representation, linguistic or cultural prejudice, and so forth. This unwanted and inappropriate 'branding' can create such severe discomfort that it becomes a contributing factor in violent separatism.

Even (or perhaps especially) outlawed organizations depend on the cloud of trust as well as the cloud of appeal in order to attract new members and support for their causes; brand management is consequently just as important to an organization like Al Qaeda as it is to a corporation like Apple. Broadcasting trust and appeal is the lifeblood of such organizations, which depend entirely on long-distance effects created through formal and informal networks of associates, since person-to-person 'selling' from the core of the organization itself directly to its 'consumer base' is only available in very limited forms.

The fact that branding is a vital component of the strategies of Al Qaeda and its associated organizations is clearly shown by Daniel Kimmage of Radio Free Europe in his recent analysis of jihadist media.[4] As Kimmage says, 'Jihadist media are attempting to mimic a "traditional" structure in order to boost credibility and facilitate message control. While conventional wisdom holds that jihadist media have been quick to exploit technological innovations to advance their cause, they are moving toward a more structured approach based on consistent branding and quasi-official media entities. Their reasons for doing so appear to be a desire to boost the credibility of their products and ensure message control. In line with this strategy, the daily flow of jihadist media that appears on the internet is consistently and systematically branded.'

What Al Qaeda has been able to achieve over the last eight or nine years must surely rank as one of the most effective brand-building campaigns in history. The extraordinary global branding effect achieved by a small, heavily constrained, initially unknown and relatively under-resourced body deserves examination. It seems as if Al Qaeda has deliberately sought to harness the branding power of nations and populations much larger and more influential than itself, and pit them against each other. Thus, Al Qaeda is not merely an organization that depends on its own brand to magnify its importance, attract recruits and gain attention; it also deploys the brands of other players in order to achieve its aims. The real purpose of the 9/11 attacks was, arguably, to stir up mistrust and enmity between the 'West' and 'Islam', and in order to achieve this effect, Al Qaeda used the huge energy of religious and political beliefs and global public opinion to 'slingshot' its message into orbit, just as NASA uses the gravitational fields of other planets to send its spacecraft into the outer reaches of the solar system, despite these craft having nowhere near enough onboard power to travel such distances. Thus, Al Qaeda is a brander as well as a brand, and this is the secret of its inordinate influence.

The collateral damage caused by the endless cycle of hostility between Islam and the West doesn't, of course, start or finish with the negative branding of Muslims against non-Muslims and vice versa: it has also inflicted enormous damage on the brand images of many nations, thus constraining their ability to engage productively in international trade and international relations for many years to come.

When Iran was included as a 'guest nation' in the 4th Quarter of the 2006 Nation Brands Index, for example, some of the extent of this collateral damage was revealed. Iran's scores were the lowest overall on every dimension, and indeed for every question in the survey except the two concerned with cultural and historical heritage. Even on these questions, Iran was ranked 35th and 36th out of 38 countries measured.

That one of the world's oldest and most important continuous civilizations, representing six millennia of culture and learning, can today be ranked virtually at the bottom of the world's leading nations for its cultural and historical heritage, lower even than countries whose civilizations are mere centuries old, must surely give pause for thought. The power of political and ideological discord to wipe millennia of achievement from the memory of humanity in a matter of decades is a terrifying power indeed.

As I mentioned earlier, people may rebel against the brand image imposed on them by external opinion as a result of their membership of a certain group: it is to be hoped that the respectable and moderate citizens of countries like Iran and Pakistan might one day rebel against their being branded – through the efforts of their own leaders, the ignorance of the media, or the propaganda of Western governments – as militant fundamentalists.

This is the tyranny of public opinion, the coarsening effect of the simple shorthands we all use in order to sum up complex groups of people. Trying to understand and, if possible, to have some influence over these shorthands is the real justification for the existence of the discipline: competitive identity is, as I have often said, legitimate self-defence against the tyranny of ignorance.

This impatience with the coarsening effect of the 'group brand' is also part of the reason why political parties find it harder and harder to create and sustain membership, at least in stable and prosperous democracies. As countries get richer, and most basic needs are answered, then the strong practical distinctions between political ideologies begin to fade, and the issues that motivate people tend to become more subtle, more personal, more variable, and less susceptible to the broad theologies of party politics: when everybody is middle-class, distinctions like 'left wing' and 'right wing' cease to have much meaning. In such circumstances, it is not surprising if voters dislike being branded as subscribers to an entire belief system when their actual views on different issues may range widely across the traditional political spectrum. Nobody wants to be branded as a 'conservative' or a 'liberal' if this means traducing their views on a large proportion of the issues that they care about, and until the arrival of a new generation of political brands that communicate in a more sophisticated and more nuanced way the concerns of modern voters, it seems likely that democratic participation will continue to decline.

However, the simplifying effect of a group brand may be, for certain people at certain times in their lives, precisely what they want, and the ability to hide one's complex personal identity behind the coarse narrative of a branded group can be very appealing. This is why rebellious adolescents are so often attracted to the simple, potent brand images of gangs, supporters' clubs, street fashions and fundamentalist sects: the desire to sublimate the difficulty and complexity of an emerging personality into something clear, shared and straightforward, doubtless lies behind much behaviour of this sort. The syndrome tends to be more widespread and less age-specific in those cultures characterized by anthropologists as 'communitarian' or 'collectivist', but is found to some degree in all societies.

It is never pleasant to have one's national identity defined or caricatured by others, especially when they have loud voices. There is a good example of this in the United Kingdom: because the British 'identity' favoured in popular American culture appears to be a nostalgic fantasy based mainly on James Bond films, there is a tendency not just for Hollywood portrayals of Britain to follow this stereotype (e.g. *Austin Powers*), but for British productions to follow suit (e.g. *Four Weddings and a Funeral, Love Actually, Notting Hill, Johnny English*). The problem is that these 'alien' portrayals are never very far removed from reality: they are reality seen through a slightly different cultural lens than the nation's own self-view, and are thus very hard to combat, or even distinguish from the 'real thing'. Consequently, there is a danger that after repeated exposure to such interpretations of identity, the population of the country itself may start to play along with the portrayal, especially if it is a beguiling and popular one. An English friend of mine recently admitted to finding himself 'putting on a Hugh Grant voice' whenever he visited America, because it seems to make people like him so much.

There is always the possibility that groups whose identity is fragile (an emerging nation, an émigré community, a minority group), might be tempted to fall in with an interpretation of their identity that is favoured by more powerful groups, especially if it appears to give them a clearer, more robust and more likeable status in the world and in their host countries.

This can be considered a good rather than a bad thing, and a useful step-up on the way to forging a richer and truer identity in the longer term. If the 'manufactured identity' provides clarity and acceptance, even for trivial or false reasons, that is an important preliminary to achieving real acceptance in the long run. The important thing is that the temporary identity doesn't become 'rusted into place' and that it serves purely as the first stage in a longer and more rewarding conversation between peoples. One can see the Australians currently grappling with a grossly simplified Hollywood interpretation of their national identity (such as that portrayed in *Crocodile Dundee*) as they try to move it towards something more complex, more nuanced, more true and more useful to their aims.

But the phenomenon has a mirror-image that is less positive. Today in many Western European countries, one can witness many discontented or alienated young Muslims 'playing along' with the identity provided for them by the media (the narrative being 'willing recruits for extremism'). This is an age-old problem: in seeking to understand a phenomenon such as religious fundamentalism, commentators discuss it in public and in the media, and in this way a consensus is reached and the phenomenon becomes named, and branded; branding makes it more real, more powerful and more accessible. This brand, once created, is then perceived to offer an identity to certain groups within the population who feel the lack of a strong identity of their own. Unable or unwilling to identify with their parents' or grandparents' national identity, and unwilling or unwelcome participants in the identity of the country where they are born and raised, they feel naked and unbranded. 'Willing recruits for extremism' may be a negative brand, but any brand is better than none, and young men especially tend to be drawn towards riskier and more dangerous or antisocial identities:

young Muslims are offered this suit of clothing by public opinion, and not surprisingly, some of them choose to put it on.

This unwitting process of branding population groups also serves to widen the gulf between the 'our brand' of mainstream society and the 'their brand' of the disaffected. This is precisely the function of brands in the commercial marketplace: to put clear water between one product and another and build an incontrovertible separateness of identity which is the prerequisite of strong loyalty. In a competitive commercial marketplace, it is entirely desirable; in a society seeking to become healthily diverse and tolerant, it is horribly dangerous.

Reputation in one form or another is the underlying currency of our modern world, and in consequence is just as much a part of the solution to these problems as their cause.

There's no question that the ideas and techniques which are explored and discussed in the pages of this book are, in the main, competitive techniques: competitive identity is attractive to many countries because it appears to offer them a way to improve their prospects for trade, aid, economic development, political influence and general respect from the international community. Ultimately, however, competitive identity isn't an entirely selfish pursuit, even if it is usually driven by national self-interest: so many of today's problems are caused by people knowing too little about other places and other groups of people, by the eternal human habit of reducing those places and groups to the level of a convenient, superficial, and often negative brand, that any approach which helps to promote a fuller and richer understanding of humanity and its populations and cultures must surely produce societal benefits in the longer term.

The deliberate use of branding effects to turn people and nations against each other is, indeed, a powerful tool in the wrong hands, but it is equally capable of producing the opposite effect. I hope that this book can play some part in developing and disseminating the skills which will enable countries and coalitions of countries to do the latter.

CHAPTER 3

National Identity: Cause or Effect?

If only there were a forum for such debates within the emerging discipline of competitive identity, one of the hottest debates would surely revolve around the question of whether national reputation is better influenced by operating on causes, or effects.

The 'logos and slogans' school of thought, deriving from the commercial selling arts, is premised on the belief that perceptions of places can be directly influenced by communications: in other words, that people can be persuaded through one form of rhetoric or another to alter their opinions about countries, cities or regions.

The 'policy-based' approach that I have always recommended holds that a purely communications-based approach is little more than futile propaganda, since countries and cities are profoundly different from products and corporations, and that the reputations of places can only be meaningfully influenced by addressing their root causes.

Much research suggests that the images of places are largely a matter of 'reality with delay', something rather solidly built over many decades, not something volatile and transient that can be pushed around at will by external agents.

People, naturally, like to own their beliefs and seldom take kindly to having them challenged or manipulated by others – perhaps least of all by foreign governments. The art of changing those beliefs, therefore, lies in altering the phenomena which give rise to the beliefs. In this way, the 'audience' will still own its own belief, and feel – quite justifiably – that it has arrived at it itself, independently.

Believing that advertising or marketing campaigns can change international perceptions of countries is, in fact, just as naïve and just as lazy as trying to make somebody lose weight by massaging the parts of their body that look too fat. It doesn't work because the fat is beneath the surface, and no amount of pummelling will get it out. One has to change the sources of nutrition that created the fat in the first place: diet and exercise are the only things that work, and they take time as well as effort, a sincere commitment to changed behaviour.

One of the few ways in which it is possible to change people's opinions directly is through genuine dialogue, by means of persuasion. There is, however, no forum available to countries for such a dialogue: the international media, where most 'place branding' attempts are carried out, only offers one-way communication. And despite its *technical* potential for two-way communication, the internet doesn't do much to overcome this problem: rather than providing real dialogue between countries and international public opinion, it really only provides a space for the recipients of 'official' communications to share and debate their responses to those (one-way) communications. Even when government ministers do find the time and the courage to participate personally in online discussions of their policies, the effects are very limited: here, the basic problem isn't one of technology but of numbers. No amount of technology can overcome the simple impossibility of a handful of people having a meaningful debate with many millions of people. I don't say it's not worth trying, but genuine dialogue of this sort is hard enough *within* a given country, let alone on an international scale.

Even if a country can occasionally speak with something like a single voice, international public opinion can never and will never do so. Perhaps the one exception to this rule is cultural relations, which can develop, with time and skill and patience, into a form of true dialogue between peoples: but it is slow, expensive, and strictly limited by the number of people it can incorporate into its programmes.

'Dialogue', in any case, gives the wrong idea: what cultural relations can hope to achieve is a wide range of multiple and very diverse conversations between peoples, and this is infinitely more valuable.

Devising a 'brand strategy' for a country is the easy part of competitive identity. Most people with a basic understanding of trade, culture, economics, international relations and a little imagination could happily spend a few interesting hours dreaming up a 'visionary' strategy for any country, if they understand that country's aims, assets and challenges well enough. And if that person chooses to pursue a communications-based approach to executing the strategy, it is equally fun and easy to dream up a range of media campaigns to present the strategy to the world. But you can't implement that strategy by telling the world about it, any more than a stand-up comedian can make an audience laugh by standing up and telling them how funny he is. The art of changing people's minds shouldn't be confused with teaching people the phrases you want to hear them use. People are not parrots.

The policy-based approach of competitive identity is far more challenging, since implementation consists of *proving* the vision, rather than just communicating it. This invariably requires a substantial change of culture within and around government, vastly improved coordination between the private and public sectors, and creating a substantial commitment to change amongst the population of the country.

Turning the strategy into an agent of change within the country is without doubt the most challenging aspect of competitive identity, and simplistic parallels with corporations and their efforts to encourage the workforce to 'live the brand' don't help much to resolve this dilemma. I have in the past also been guilty of talking enthusiastically about the need for the 'whole population to live the brand' without really considering what this means in practical terms. It is hard enough encouraging the employees of a corporation to subscribe to the values, goals and desired behaviours of the organization that pays their salaries, let alone doing this on a national scale, and under the aegis of a social contract rather than a contract of employment. If it were really possible for a political leader to unite a majority of the population into a common set of beliefs and a common pattern of behaviours without resorting to despotism and coercion, then all elections would be a foregone conclusion and democratic opposition would lose its *raison d'être*.

Nonetheless, it is clear that if a country is to change enough to alter its international reputation, this is unthinkable without the support of the population; and to understand the essential nature of the population is a prerequisite to eliciting its support.

But national identity is nearly always a vexed and elusive subject, perhaps especially in newer, poorer nations, or those with unresolved conflicts – the very nations that would benefit most from exercising some influence over their reputations.

In every country where I have worked during the last ten years, I have met and debated for hours with writers, academics and philosophers whose subject is national identity; some of them have spent a lifetime studying the question; and yet they are often the first to admit that they are scarcely any closer to any firm 'answers' on the subject than the most casual observer.

In many cases, it is more fruitful to 'change the subject' from these ultimately circular arguments, and attempt to find consensus – and, more importantly, inspiration and stimulation – in a national narrative that is based on a shared dream for the future rather than a shared interpretation of the past or the present. In other words, it is possible for nations to represent themselves in terms of the places they mean to become, the direction they choose, and the values that this implies about their people: they can tell a story about where they are going, not where they have come from, or where they are now.

There is at least one distinguished precedent for a country building its international identity on the basis of its aspirations for the future, rather than its achievements in the past: the United States sold itself to the world as a project, indeed an experiment, for more than two centuries, and gained enormous admiration and goodwill around the world for doing so.

Time and time again, in my discussions in developing countries about national identity, I find that people are always keen participants, but their manner is frequently agitated and troubled, their language conflictual and, if I am honest, relatively little progress is made during these discussions even though the content is most interesting. However, as soon as discussions move on to the question of the country's future, the participants visibly brighten; their contributions become more constructive and imaginative, and it is obvious that their emotions and intellects are not just engaged but also stimulated and excited.

It's impossible not to conclude that many developing nations find themselves at an interesting, important, perhaps critical moment in their history at the close of this decade. The simple creed of economic growth represented by the Washington consensus has provided significant momentum across many sectors of society in many of these countries, but as more people become more accustomed to the fruits of their new wealth, a loss of certainty and a sense of disappointment have unmistakably started to set in.

Many of those who have benefited from the growth of the last decades now appear to be asking, 'Is material wealth really worth the sacrifice of so much quality of life?' For those who have not yet achieved a measurable improvement in living standards and disposable income, the sense of impatience is palpable. Their question is: 'When are things going to feel different?'

There is often a commonly expressed view that many people have achieved a remarkable and palpable improvement in their lives but are somehow unable to acknowledge it. They've never had it so good but their question is 'What am I struggling for?'

Many surveys have been carried out during the last few years which show that striving for wealth, and achieving it, does bring a sense of purpose and even happiness, but only up to a certain point. Over a certain level of income, happiness, health, life expectancy and fulfilment level off; the struggle, the sacrifices and the constant hankering after a vague and ill-defined objective which forever moves further away ultimately outweigh the pleasures of anticipation and the satisfaction of what one has achieved so far. In many of the countries where I have worked during the last five or six years, in many sectors of society, this point appears to have been reached.

If one grows up in a society where accumulating material wealth is truly the cultural foundation of that society, the group creed, then this sense of emptiness is broadly tolerable, mainly because there's nothing much else on offer. But in countries where the neo-liberal creed is a relatively recent foreign implant, which conflicts with other world views and values, that sense of unfulfilment is likely to be more prevalent and more troubling.

Leaving aside the question of economic growth as a 'national project' and the fulfilment or lack of fulfilment that it brings, most people need a scheme, a sense that they know where they are heading and what they are struggling for. Unless society has some kind of shared goal, and unless that goal is in some measure inspiring, it tends to drift, and disappointment, impatience, emptiness or even depression will unavoidably set in. All groups of people, whether one is speaking of a small company or a large country, need a sense of collective purpose, and good leadership is very largely about providing this.

Perhaps the idea of competitive identity is just what many developing countries need: a chance to 'change the subject' by focusing on their position in the world rather than the country's own meaning for itself, and a chance to build a new vision for a shared future, to define the country's goals not in terms of a culturally alien economic model but according to the values and beliefs of the population itself.

Growth for the sake of growth, as Edward Abbey famously said, is the logic of the cancer cell. It is wholly inadequate as a basis for providing social cohesion, common purpose, progress and meaning to people's lives. The current global financial and economic crisis has only served to emphasize the centrality of this question – and to underline the universal significance of the dilemmas that so many developing countries are struggling with today.

The irony in all this is that many of the values and assets which so many developing countries are in the process of discarding because they seem irrelevant to the struggle for modernization and growth, are precisely those values and assets which the 'first world' is finally beginning to value most: their respect for and closeness to traditional culture and values; their respect for and closeness to nature; strong family and societal cohesion; a real sense of the poetic in daily life; a respect for culture and learning.

To put it brutally, many third-world countries run the risk of becoming trapped in the role of second-rate, second-world country, still chasing the dreams of modernity and prosperity which the first world is just now beginning to question. Instead of playing to their strengths as a 'niche offering', many emerging nations are still running a very twentieth-century race which, truthfully, only countries with large economies, large armies and large populations could ever win.

One of the great benefits of globalization, and the rapid transformation of the world from global battleground to global marketplace, is that it enables smaller countries to find a profitable niche, and compete on the basis of their cultural, environmental, imaginative and human qualities rather than on raw power. We live in an age which, for the first time in history, provides real opportunities for developing countries, but those countries need the knowledge to play by the new rules.

And the loss of identity isn't merely an unfortunate side-effect of growth: for smaller countries, identity is the *indispensable means by which they will achieve growth*. Countries that aren't strong need to be interesting – they need to exercise some power of attraction if they cannot exercise compulsion, and the source of that attraction can only be their unique, individual identity, their culture, their history, their land, their traditions, their genius and their imagination. This is what competitive identity is all about.

Can a country achieve sustainable growth whilst reducing its carbon footprint and without harming its environment? Can a culture follow capitalism without losing its moral compass? Can a society benefit from immigration without losing its distinctive identity? Can technology and poetry, art and science coexist and even collaborate in the same society? Can social justice and equality grow even faster than the economy? Can a wealthy society feed the souls as well as the bodies of its people? Can a people grasp the benefits of modernity without sacrificing what it values most from its past? In short, can a country move forwards without leaving what it values behind?

These are the central dilemmas of modernity, and it is no coincidence that it they are also the central questions of competitive identity for developing nations. Our age needs a new model and a new ethos of development and progress: and the first countries that can prove the viability of such models are assured of gaining as much in reputation as they gain in prosperity.

CHAPTER 4

Should Places Have Simple Images?

There is a basic question about the images of places which has seldom been addressed in the literature, and which remains largely unresolved: do places benefit more from having a clear, simple image, or is it preferable for them to have a rich, complex and even contradictory image? Societies are intrinsically complex and contradictory phenomena, so why should any country attempt to alter or disguise this fact in the way it represents itself and is perceived by outsiders?

The question leads to some fundamental issues about the theory and practice of competitive identity; indeed, it challenges the very idea of applying brand theory to the development of places.

Brands in the commercial sphere tend to opt unequivocally for projecting a clear and simple image. Of course, any corporation that is lucky and successful enough to have maintained its brand for generations may find that the brand image, over time, becomes richer and more complex; but branding is essentially seen as a process of reduction. The laser-like clarity of a single, distinctive positioning is often described as the product's only chance of cutting through the indifference of the consumer, the chaos of the marketplace and the clutter of the media. For decades, commercial brands have followed the prevailing wisdom and sought to reduce their 'essence' down to a single promise to the consumer.

I have long argued that places are exactly the opposite, and that this is one of the main reasons why commercial branding practice doesn't apply in any straightforward way to their management or promotion: good sense suggests, and research tends to confirm, that richness and complexity are valuable image attributes for any country, city or region. This is primarily because the image must be able to embrace and support the wide variety of industrial, cultural and political activity which countries and cities are likely to engage in. It's difficult to imagine any single 'positioning' for a country which could span all the activities of its private and public sectors, without being so bland and generic as to be useless as a distinguishing narrative.

Equally, the external 'audience' of the country, whether considered as tourists, investors, business visitors, allies, consumers of its exports, immigrants or participants in cultural exchange, must be able to find a 'promise' that matches their engagement with the country, irrespective of their own cultural viewpoint and their own sectoral interest, and at any point in time. The idea of a single promise that can embrace such a wide variety of product offerings and consumer needs seems almost absurd.

Moreover, a rich and nuanced national image acts as an insurance policy against failure or a negative consumer experience of some aspect of the country, its people or its products: this, for example, is why America's image incorporates deeply unpopular foreign policy alongside much-loved popular culture and products, and is still held in overall high esteem by many publics abroad.

However, acquiring a rich, tolerant, nuanced and complete perception of another country takes time, and requires a certain commitment on the part of the perceiver: she or he has to *learn* the country, and this surely cannot take place in a passive way, simply as a consequence of the 'single shot' of conventional marketing and branding techniques. The visitor, investor or consumer has to *want* to learn about a place in order to arrive at a fuller and richer understanding of it.

Taken in its most literal sense, the need to learn the country is the reason why working on national image through educational support programmes in foreign schools can be so effective: children who study another country at school are likely to retain a positive bias for that country which could last a lifetime.

It was in an effort to resolve this dilemma of simplicity and richness that I originally proposed the idea of nation brand as signpost:

The definition of brand as shorthand or signpost for value, or quality, or equity, is a useful one: in other words, you don't attempt to pack all meaning into a single proposition or slogan, or jump the gun on the time it takes for a consumer to 'learn' the complex product, but be content with a sign which can stand for, and later refer accurately back to, the whole experience, once it is more familiar to the consumer. One has to have the wisdom and patience to accept that this sign will not be wholly meaningful to the consumer at the start, but it is a vessel which will become more and more replete with meaning as meaning is absorbed.

...

Simplification has a tendency to reduce appeal, since so much of the ultimate appeal of a country is its richness and complexity. The true art of branding is distillation: the art of extracting the concentrated essence of something complex, so that its complexity can always be extracted back out of the distillate, but it remains portable and easily memorable. The distillate, rather than actually attempting to contain all the detail of the country in question, is simply the common thread, the genetic constant, which underlies the basic commonality between the different parts of the brand.[5]

It is typical for less well-known countries trying to establish an international profile that they will start with a signpost brand of this sort: it is the sharp point of their image which enables them to penetrate consumer consciousness and add their country's name to the list of candidate countries in the consumer's mind.

Indeed, there is probably some close equivalent for places of the classic marketing notion of the 'evoked set', a theory which argues that prospective purchasers never hold a shortlist of more than a small number of items in consideration at any one time. It would be a worthwhile research project to try and determine whether the evoked set theory does indeed hold true for places: as tourist destinations, business travel destinations, investment locations, and even as political allies, cultural partners and country of origin for products and services. If so, the implications are striking: for any country to stand a chance of being selected in one of these categories, it is not enough for them to improve their image; they need to force their way into the evoked set.

Such countries, having used a deliberately simplified brand promise to establish their presence in the evoked set and register in the consciousness of the audience, can then gradually proceed to a widening of the discourse and a more nuanced 'conversation' with their multiple target groups.

Better-known countries, on the other hand, might already be within the evoked set and have little interest in developing a single 'promise' (and little chance of doing so without compromising the significance and breadth of their image and identity), but will want to invest more in the activities that typically widen and deepen existing awareness of their full offering: cultural relations, educational activities and exchanges, cultural tourism, etc.

Some countries might be faced with the need to sharpen *and* broaden their image at the same time for different publics or in different sectors, as economic patterns change. Wealthy, developed European nations, for example, may need to broaden and enrich their profiles within Europe and North America, but find that they are much less well-known in their emerging target markets of China, India, Russia and Brazil, where the task is really one of introduc-ing the brand; and a simpler, single promise is then far more appropriate.

In all cases, this kind of reductive, signpost branding should only be considered as a temporary measure, designed to get a country to register on the radar of indifferent or ignorant audiences. Such a brand is comparable to the point of an ice-axe, the purpose of which is to achieve traction on the steep ice-face of people's limited attention and interest in other countries. As soon as feasible, the relationship must be broadened, and marketing or selling must give way to teaching and discussing; projection must give way to engagement; monologue must be replaced by dialogue. But no dialogue is possible without first creating the desire for that dialogue in the interlocutor.

Moving away as soon as possible from the signpost phase of competitive identity is essential not least because there are real dangers associated with the attempt to whet a country's identity into a single-minded, potent and functioning brand with international reach. Such an exercise, as I have often argued, runs the risk of devaluing the essential dignity of places; of diminishing the diversity of culture, race, history and activities of the place; of creating an undesirable level of Foucaultian governmentality;[6] of excluding certain sectors of business or community from the benefit of the positive image; and of holding the country hostage to a narrow promise which later circumstances might invalidate. In many ways, this kind of branding is the conceptual opposite of democracy; it is also extremely risky.

Indeed, as I mentioned in the Introduction, the deliberate branding of places looks more like a problem than a solution in the longer term. 'Branding' in this sense is what public opinion does, reducing the richness of the nation (richness being a component of its essential dignity) to the level of a naïve shorthand. It is not what governments should deliberately try to do, 'playing to the gallery' and pandering to the ignorance of public opinion. What responsible governments *ought* to do is enrich and improve, or at least maintain and protect, the nation's good name, that most valuable national asset with which they have been entrusted for the term of their office.

The argument that good place images are rich and complex has usually been espoused, even if not expressed in quite these terms, by the proponents and practitioners of cultural relations, both in the context of national image building and bilateral relationship building. The experience of countries which have successfully practised cultural relations over many years shows that consistent, mutual cultural exchange does eventually create an environment where respect and tolerance flourish, and this undoubtedly also favours increased trade in skills, knowledge, products, capital and people. People who understand each other tend to get on better, and people who get on better tend to trade with each other more frequently, more freely and with greater mutual profit.

The real challenge is opening the door to dialogue in the first place. Overcoming the essential lack of interest in a foreign country may in some cases be a matter of *disrupting* the audience's indifference, prejudice or expectations. The problem faced by most countries is not that they lack good things to say about themselves, or even that they don't say or do good things often enough: it's usually that people just aren't paying attention, and don't see why they should.

This is the main reason why I have so often insisted on the inappropriateness of marketing communications for enhancing, creating or altering national image. Such forms of advertising work, and are acceptable, when one is offering something that is for sale to people who are, at least potentially, interested in what one is selling. In place branding one is promoting something that isn't for sale to people who are almost certainly not interested. Under such circumstances, the whole panoply of marketing communications is fatally compromised.

Governments that want to 'brand' their countries should therefore not ask the question 'what can we say to make our country famous?', but 'what can we do to make our country relevant?' Instead of asking how they can charm or coerce people into admiring their country, they should ask themselves *why* people in other countries should even think about their country in the first place. And if there honestly is no good reason why people should think about that country, and if a good reason can't be created, then the idea of nation branding should simply be dropped, and the government should accept that their destiny, at least for the time being, is not to be famous or admired outside their own neighbourhood or region, just quietly effective. And in many cases, there may be nothing wrong with having a low profile: being a 'famous country' is no sort of panacea.

The all-important question of relevance is discussed in more detail in Chapter 12, but for the time being it's important to emphasize that making the country relevant to the audience involves a number of notions which are all too often left out of the place branding discourse. The first of these – which incidentally happens to be one of the basic rules of marketing – is to base one's strategy on a clear analysis of the perceptions, needs, habits and aspirations of one's target audience; indeed, to treat this as a more important consideration than the product offering itself. It is rare indeed that governmental place branding teams look anywhere except inwards, and they frequently end up simply describing the place, repeating long and carefully-prepared lists of its attributes and achievements. This is classic bad marketing, as it provides no 'reason to buy', and by failing to demonstrate any understanding of the target audience, creates no empathy or sympathy with them, and fails to open a dialogue.

Another classic error is the failure to offer the target audience anything in return for its attention; again, this is classic bad marketing, as it makes the fundamental error of assuming that the consumer is as interested in the 'product' as its 'producer' is.

Part of the reason why cultural relations is one of the few demonstrably effective forms of place branding is because it offers some pleasure in return for the consumer's attention: by proposing artistic or intellectual stimulation, the country both delights its audience and pays in advance for the respect and interest of that audience. Bearing cultural gifts in this way gives pleasure to the recipient, and at the same time burnishes the reputation of the giver.

So powerful and so effective is this kind of transaction, countries increasingly now recognize that these exercises of 'soft power' are anything but soft. The benefits are measurable, tangible, and considerably more cost-effective than coercion. There is, currently, an explosion in the quantity of art and culture being exhibited and consumed around the world, and although it is hard to measure, the increase might just as well be supply-driven as demand-driven: rather than revealing a gratifying increase in the cultural appetites and sensibilities of populations, it may simply demonstrate how many governments are beginning to realize the tremendous power of cultural diplomacy for achieving their foreign policy objectives via the general population, rather than via official government channels.

Yet many people, perhaps in particular those who revere 'traditional' diplomacy, are keenly skeptical about the whole notion of national image. Michel Girard makes a cogent argument against this modern preoccupation:

> *...when one is overly possessed by communication of images, all productive energy and attention is being channelled outside the substance of the problem one is meant to solve. In negotiation, it is quite often helpful to exercise some discretion, even outright confidentiality, as political matters cannot be pushed towards quick solutions. To mediate successfully, there must be a third party role – one possessing the ability to maintain a front of temporary secrecy for the sake of the antagonists' building of trust through stating sincere positions and facilitating realistic bargaining and so on. But*

when the third party is running for popularity concurrently with keeping the negotiations onboard, diplomatic and media purposes will cross. The result is a kind of soft and anodyne diplomacy. In other words, a diplomacy which does not want to hurt anybody, and tries only to multiply opportunities to improve one's image.[7]

This observation cuts right to the heart of the question of place image, and yet seems to miss a fundamental point. To characterize all 'branding' or 'public relations' or 'advertising' (terms which Girard uses more or less interchangeably) as inherently deceptive practices, unfailingly borne of a desire to manipulate the perceptions of the public, is facile, and curtails what should be a longer and more profound enquiry. Not all governments use communications in order to lay claim to motivations which are different from their real ones, and desiring a particular image for one's country isn't necessarily incompatible with doing things for the 'right' reasons. Nothing could be more natural than to desire that one's country enjoys the reputation it deserves; to ensure that it deserves it; and to ensure that it enjoys it.

The best possible reason for wishing to present a particular national image is that it is both fair and true; the desire is simply to be properly understood, rather than allow one's country to remain forever the victim of an out-of-date cliché, truly 'branded' by public ignorance. The experience from my own practice is that very many governments, far from trying to present an idealized or invented 'brand' for themselves, are in fact trying to shed the 'brand' which public opinion, or public ignorance, has foisted on them.

Some would claim, myself included, that hoodwinking international public opinion is, in any case, almost impossible, since no government begins to exercise any meaningful influence over the multiple channels of communication that publics have access to. As I have often said, one of the benign effects of the globalization of media is that it has rendered propaganda anachronistic, a virtual impossibility.

Far from being incompatible, the art of good branding and the art of good leadership are, at heart, indistinguishable, since both are fundamentally concerned with being true to one's core values. Branding teaches the importance of having a set of firm beliefs and values, a clarity of purpose, which unfailingly drives one's decisions; in other words, integrity. Branding, at its best, is a technique for achieving integrity, and reaping the reputational benefits of integrity.

The importance of clarity, interestingly, was raised by another speaker at the same conference where Girard made the observations quoted above. Quentin Peel, a journalist, said the following:

> *Margaret Thatcher had a clear line. John Major had a total muddle. A tremendous amount of spin-doctoring went on to try and put some clarity in this muddle, but in the end nobody wanted to know because his policies were a complete confusion. So, whether you liked the policies or not she had a policy and it was saleable and people wanted to hear it. He had confusion and in the end they just walked away. The lesson of all this is that it is not worth telling the public if you have a bad policy or a muddled policy. Have a clear policy and then you do not have to sell it in the end.*[8]

Although Peel is unsurprisingly suspicious of the use of public relations by governments to push a particular line to the media, he acknowledges that what really matters to the media, and consequently to public opinion, is clarity; and clarity is precisely what any good brand strategy will attempt to deliver – both internally and externally.

What if brand management were ultimately all about developing clear policies that clearly resonate with one's fundamental values and beliefs? What if branding were more about being truthful than being mendacious? What if branding were more about good governance and good leadership than presentation or rhetoric? What if branding were more about learning how to be true to oneself than how to lie to other people?

Some might think that the espousal of branding techniques by governments is a symptom of weakness and dishonesty, a sign that the government is driven by public opinion, but in fact it can be, and should be, exactly the opposite: it's a sign that the government desires the country and its policies to be driven by its true identity. It's the lack of a set of core principles and identity which creates poor and muddled policies *and* poor reputation. Inner certainty creates good policies, clear behaviour, and a good reputation.

The way in which the images of places is formed can be expressed by the simple model:

IDENTITY – BEHAVIOUR – IMAGE

Who you are determines how you behave; how you behave determines how you are perceived. Competitive identity, when properly understood, is a system that respects the power of integrity above all else, and recognizes that only perfect integrity can sway public opinion.

CHAPTER 5

Sketches of National Image and Identity

Pakistan and Mexico

Talking about Pakistan's international image may sound irrelevant, even absurd, at a more than usually troubled time in the country's history, but the simple fact is that every country on earth depends on its good name in order to achieve its aims in the globally connected world we live in today.

At some point in the future, when things have stabilized a little, Pakistan will find that its ability to interact effectively and profitably with other countries will depend to a considerable extent on its good or bad image; its ability to lure back its most talented emigrés and stem the tide of those leaving to study and work abroad; its ability to attract business and leisure visitors as well as foreign investment; the quality of its engagements with other governments and multilateral agencies: all of these transactions will be considerably easier if Pakistan's reputation improves, and they will prove a constant, uphill struggle if its reputation remains as weak and negative as it has become today.

With daily violence, a bitter struggle against insurgent elements along the Afghan border, and constant political and social upheaval, the international image of Pakistan is in tatters, and is probably the last thing on the mind of Pakistan's government as they fight for political survival and ascendancy over the Taleban. But there will come a day when the country needs to think again about restoring its damaged reputation: and the longer the country remains in free-fall, the harder a task this will be.

The Mexican government probably wasn't primarily concerned with its international reputation either, when the southern state of

Tabasco lay partly under water in 2008 or when swine flu threatened to develop into a global pandemic in early 2009: at such moments, its main concerns were rather more practical and immediate. But when major natural disasters happen, people often do worry that it will damage their country's international interests by spoiling its image, and they are usually wrong. Most of my research suggests that the things which happen *to* a country (such as natural disasters, terrorist attacks or epidemics) seldom affect people's perceptions of that country in any profound or lasting way: what changes the image of a country far more is how the country *responds* to such crises, and what the government, the people or the companies in that country *do* – especially when it has an impact on people in other countries.

The population of Pakistan quite rightly feel that they are as little to blame for their country's current woes as the people of Mexico: but they are nonetheless likely to suffer the consequences of them for very much longer. Mexico will recover from floods and flu, people will rebuild their lives and their communities, and life will return to something like normal for the majority of those affected; before very long, world opinion will focus on another disaster, and will forget the Tabasco floods and swine flu, just as it has begun to forget Pakistan's devastating earthquakes of 2005.

But because Pakistan's present troubles are man-made, their effect on the world's perceptions of the country will persist, and Pakistan will struggle for decades to present itself to the world as a responsible, trustworthy ally and partner in trade, tourism and politics. Acts of God can harm a country in many ways: but it is acts of men that cause the most lasting damage.

Kenya

An article from the Nairobi Business Daily in 2008 told how the 'Brand Kenya' initiative, despite a great deal of goodwill, failed to get off the ground. Various reasons were given for the project's lack of momentum, including the absence of sufficient political will: it is certainly true that unless such projects have the sustained and personal backing of the head of government and, preferably, the head of state, they are unlikely to go very far or last very long. Without such authority and commitment, there is little incentive for the various stakeholders to collaborate, and they will soon revert to 'business as usual'.

What was striking about the article, however, was the unquestioned assumption that a lack of funds was the real reason for the failure of the project. Various people were quoted, mentioning staggering sums of money, and pointing out that these sums were inadequate because they were less than the average corporation spends on advertising, and therefore well below the minimum required to 'brand' a country.

This seems to be missing the point. Countries can't simply buy their way into a positive 'brand image' – especially if, like most African countries, their current image is very negative or very weak. Every country that has ever succeeded in noticeably improving its reputation – South Africa, Ireland, Japan, Germany, Spain – has done so as a result of economic or political progress. The advertising and PR campaigns which occasionally accompany these 'branding miracles' are never the cause of them, although on occasions they have been some help in making people aware, both inside the country itself and abroad, of the changes that are taking place, and thus shortening the normal lag between reality and perception. This is a classic case of confusing correlation and causality: claiming that the advertising causes the new image is like noticing that I open my umbrella whenever it starts to rain, and then hailing me as a magician because I can make it rain just by opening my umbrella.

Creating a better image for a country is often far cheaper and always infinitely harder than people imagine. It's about creating a viable yet inspirational long-term vision for the development of the country and pursuing that aim through good leadership, economic and social reform, imaginative and effective cultural and political relations, transparency and integrity, infrastructure, education, and so forth: in other words, substance. The substance is then expressed, over many years, through a series of symbolic actions which bring it memorably, effectively and lastingly to the world's attention.

Nations have brand images: that much is clear. And those brand images are extremely important to their progress in the modern world. Brand theory can be helpful in understanding those images, measuring and monitoring them, and even investigating how they have come about. But brand marketing cannot do very much to change them. Change comes from good governance, wise investment, innovation and popular support.

What created the image in the first place? Not communications. What can change the image in the future? Not communications. What Kenyans need to understand is that winning a better image is not only a matter of persuading government to get involved in the issue: it is the primary responsibility of the government, and that image is the direct consequence of the leadership and good governance given by the government – or the lack of it.

Creating a more positive national image is not a project that government needs to take an interest in. Earning a more positive national image is what good governance is all about.

Denmark

Denmark is a good example of a country which might easily fall into the trap of thinking that its national image is as good as it can be, and there's little point in worrying about it. But of course this would be a mistake, for two main reasons:

1. Denmark is well-known and highly reputed in its immediate neighbourhood, and for several centuries its good name has made commercial, cultural, social and political relations easy and pleasant within that neighbourhood. But along comes globalization, and Denmark finds that it's no longer competing and trading with its neighbours, but with countries on the other side of the world, where its history and identity are virtually unknown. Of course, Denmark has the 'Scandinavian premium' (because Scandinavia is a powerful international 'brand'), but in the countries where many of Denmark's future trading partners, tourists, consumers, strategic partners and perhaps allies will

come from – notably China, India, Brazil and Russia – the country itself is relatively unknown. Used to being well-known and respected, this is a difficult concept for Denmark to adjust to: but adjust it must.

2. Denmark's image in the global popular imagination is, like the images of most countries, rooted in its past. Its story is one of an overwhelmingly white, prosperous, Protestant population carrying on in that effective, egalitarian, social-democratic way that it has for centuries. But of course the story is no longer absolutely true, and excludes an ever larger part of the population. This way trouble lies: nobody likes living in a country which still presents itself to the world – and is regarded by the world – as the kind of country where people like them couldn't possibly live.

Denmark's image took a battering in 2007 as a result of the 'cartoons crisis', a subject I wrote about in *Competitive Identity* and elsewhere. The Nation Brands Index™ suggests that much of the fallout from this sorry episode is now over, and in most countries Denmark's ranking is as high, or indeed higher, than it was before the cartoons were published (although the Egyptian population has yet to forgive or forget the episode). But Denmark learned an important lesson from the cartoons: in today's world, countries are no longer considered as loose collections of different groups – the government, the media, businesses, ordinary people, famous people – but as single players on a global stage. If one component offends, the whole national entity is likely to be implicated. It's not fair, it's not clever and it's not logical, but it's the way public opinion works.

And this tendency of globalization to reduce the complexity and diversity of countries to simple, one-dimensional 'brands', creates enormous problems for democratic governance. It is unthinkable for a liberal, secular, democratic state in the modern world to attempt to control the actions and communications of all its stakeholders; and yet the consequences of the actions and communications of a single stakeholder, public or private, are apt to have a profound impact on the shared reputation of all.

That reputation, as Denmark discovered to its cost, is the most precious asset of a country in the age of globalization. As Iago says in Shakespeare's *Othello*,

Good name in man and woman, dear my lord,
Is the immediate jewel of their souls.
Who steals my purse steals trash; 'tis something, nothing;
'Twas mine, 'tis his, and has been slave to thousands;
But he that filches from me my good name
Robs me of that which not enriches him,
And makes me poor indeed.

(*Othello*, Act 3, scene 3, 155–161)

Shakespeare speaks of personal reputation within society, but the point is no less true of national reputation within what some people hopefully call the 'community of nations'.

Under the tyranny of international public opinion, what is diverse becomes homogeneous and what is complex becomes simple. In order to live at peace with others and tolerate or even enjoy their differences, it is essential to particularize, but the fatal tendency of humanity is always to generalize.

Italy

Italy has the seventh best national image in the world, according to the Nation Brands Index, coming top for tourism and second for culture. Its ranking is only let down by rather poor scores for business and governance, as you might expect. Italy's image is, in fact, virtually the opposite of Germany's: very strong on the 'soft' side where Germany is weak (people, landscape, culture, fashion and food brands) and weak on the 'hard' side where Germany is strong (governance, economy, engineering brands). It occurs to me that a merger between the two would probably create the strongest all-round national image on the planet.

And yet there is a worrying undercurrent when you look more closely at Italy's rankings over the last few years: not only is it the most volatile of any Top 10 country in the Index, but it is also in steady decline. Italy's rankings have dropped by 2.3% since the questionnaire of the Nation Brands Index was stabilized in the last quarter of 2005 – which may not sound much, but at this rate Italy will have a weaker image than Mexico in ten years' time.

Italy's decline looks gentle but in fact it is the third steepest of any country in the Index, apart from China, Hungary and South Korea (which, tragically, is often confused by respondents with North Korea, so one can't give its results too much credence).

In an age when it seems that every government is frantic to understand and manage its national image and compete more effectively in the global marketplace, Italy's leaders seem happy to sit back and wait. Perhaps such a wealth of landscape, culture, cuisine, history and world-famous brands creates a certain complacency. But there are competitors creeping up on all sides, and one can't help wondering just how long that bed of laurels will remain so comfortable.

It seems pretty clear to me that Italy's brand is not actually declining in absolute terms: the reason why Italy's scores are falling so fast in the Nation Brands Index is because the world is changing its mind on a number of issues, and Italy is being very gradually 'squeezed out' of the new scenario. As I've often said, country images really don't change very much; it is somewhat easier to spoil a country's image than improve it, but even that is pretty hard work.

What Italy seems to be facing is not a loss of attraction in its image, but a decline in the relevance of that image for many people. In other words, Italy could be going out of fashion.

Judging by the profiles of countries that people admire more as time passes, there are at least three areas of reputation which seem to have become critical in recent years:

1. A country's perceived environmental credentials. This is rapidly becoming a 'hygiene factor' for a country's basic acceptance into the community of nations.
2. A country's perceived competence and productivity in technology, which seems to be the standard proxy for modernity: and people, on the whole, admire modern countries.

3. A country's attractiveness as a place of learning and economic and cultural self-improvement: in other words, a destination for personal advancement.

Italy scores poorly in all three of these areas:

1. Worse than being just another country that isn't perceived to be doing very much in the area of environmentalism, it is perceived as a country with a hugely important natural and cultural heritage that isn't doing very much to look after it.
2. Italy, like Germany, is perceived as a country with *mechanical* rather than *technological* excellence: Ferraris and Fiats are great engineering products, but people are slow to accept Italy as a source of high technology (witness the difficulties faced by Olivetti when it tried to market its personal computers internationally).
3. And although Italy is a country most people would love to live in, they really only think of it as an extended holiday destination. When it comes to answering the critical question 'what's in it for me?', Italy is not perceived to offer much.

Part of the problem is the view that Italy is not to any great degree an English-speaking nation, so the prospects for internationally useful educational or work experience or qualifications are very limited.

The way to fix this, I firmly believe, has less to do with the standard of English-language teaching in Italian schools (which is admittedly poor) and more to do with the fact that English-language television is routinely dubbed into Italian rather than subtitled. Children don't spend many hours learning English at school and usually don't pay close attention: but they do spend hours a day watching television, and watching it quite closely. If a proportion of the programmes and movies they watch have English dialogue and Italian subtitles, they will learn English almost without realizing it. Certainly, most of the countries where foreign television is subtitled have higher standards of general competence in English than the countries where it's dubbed into the local language.

And a word to the cultural protectionists who would 'protect' their populations against the rising tide of Anglo-American popular culture: competence in English has no real political or cultural significance any more. English is not the language of Britain or America or Australia or anywhere else: it's the operating system of the modern world, more like Windows than Word, and if you can't use it then you can't easily participate in the international community.

Places that resist the rise of English on the grounds that it brands them as pro-American or pro-British are missing the point: it makes them globally competitive and doesn't brand them as anything in particular, except possibly as competent and modern. Oh, and there's *plenty* of good quality film and television programming made in the English language (and not all of it from Britain and America either) which will neither warp the morals of young people or destroy their native culture. A *smaller* proportion of higher quality English-language television broadcast in the original language will do far more good than the current high proportion of poor quality programming dubbed into Italian.

In the end, this final question about whether people would like to move to a country to study, live and work, is a good measure for the overall attractiveness of the place. Whatever people might think about a country's products, policies or culture, if they believe that they can improve their personal prospects by moving there, it means that they ultimately approve of the place (the United States, despite all the negative views surrounding its foreign policy and cultural and economic hegemony and the brouhaha about its failed public diplomacy, is still by a long way most people's preferred destination for education and professional development, and this is one of the main reasons why I don't believe that the country's current unpopularity is in any sense terminal).

It goes without saying that Italy's weakness in these three areas is neither absolutely deserved nor absolutely undeserved. There are plenty of great places in Italy for foreigners to study for internationally respected and relevant qualifications; some of Europe's most committed environmentalists are based in Italy; and some of Europe's most innovative, successful and highly reputed technology firms are Italian. The problem is that these facts are not feeding into the popular 'story' of Italy: they are known only by limited groups of people with specialist knowledge, and can do very little to shift the vast weight of Italy's traditional international image – the country of *la dolce vita*.

Italy's problem is that it is considered by the vast majority of people as a place that is decorative but not useful. The Italy that the world wants is full of attractive, soft, lifestyle values – it's a place where, at least in their minds, they can retreat from the troubles of the modern world – and people simply don't want that attractive myth, that imaginary refuge, 'contaminated' by the things that the rest of the world worries about. Italy wants, and needs, to work: but the world wants it to stay on holiday. And, it has to be added, with the clownish figure of Silvio Berlusconi at the helm, cracking sexist jokes and generally behaving as little like a responsible international statesman as he can contrive to do, there is little chance that this view is likely to change in the short term.

Indeed, there's not much one can do to fix any of this, at least not without wide-scale, long-term political and social reform, a prospect which with every change of government seems less and less likely.

Israel

In the third quarter of 2006, I included Israel for the first time in the NBI, as there had been more speculation than usual about the country's international image during the previous months, mainly as a result of the Israeli army's incursion into Lebanon just as the Quarter 3 NBI was being researched. At the same time, the Government of Israel announced that it would be undertaking a 'branding campaign' in an attempt to address negative perceptions of the country around the world. As Reuters reported on September 30th that year:

> *After decades of battling to win foreign support for its two-fisted policies against Arab foes, Israel is trying a new approach with a campaign aimed at creating a less warlike and more welcoming national image. Foreign Minister Tzipi Livni, who has argued that the protracted conflict with the Palestinians is sapping Israel's*

international legitimacy, this week convened diplomats and PR executives to come up with ways of 'rebranding' the country. 'When the word "Israel" is said outside its borders, we want it to invoke not fighting or soldiers, but a place that is desirable to visit and invest in, a place that preserves democratic ideals while struggling to exist,' Livni said.

The article went on to mention that the advertising agency, Saatchi and Saatchi, was helping the Israeli government free of charge in this campaign.

The Israeli government is certainly right to be concerned: the international image of the country was in very poor shape indeed, and continues to be so. Israel's brand was by a considerable margin the most negative we had ever measured in the NBI, and came bottom of the ranking on almost every question. Only Bhutan, the first 'guest country' we included in the NBI, achieved similarly low scores, but this was because very few of our respondents in the 35 countries where we run the survey had even heard of the tiny Himalayan kingdom, let alone held any firm views about it. Israel's poor scores were clearly not the result of anonymity: it is one of the most famous countries in the world.

It is in the areas of governance that Israel achieved its lowest scores. In response to one of the questions in this section of the survey, 'how strongly do you agree with the statement that this country behaves responsibly in the areas of international peace and security?', Israel scored lowest of all the 36 countries in the NBI; even the U.S. panel, otherwise one of the more positive panels towards Israel, put Israel 35th out of 36 on this question (China is last).

Russia gave Israel its highest rankings, and the views of the Russian panel were noticeably out of kilter with those of the other 35 countries polled (the only bottom ranking given to Israel by the Russian panel was for the country's natural beauty). On the question of international peace and security, Russia ranked Israel 20th overall.

One of the most significant questions in the NBI, and one which over the years I have found to be one of the best indicators of generally positive or negative feelings about countries, is the one which asks people how willing they would be to live and work for an extended period in the country. Changes in responses to this question also reflect overall changes in perceptions of the country more accurately than any other question in the survey. Here, Israel was ranked last by every panel including the Americans, and even the Russians only gave it a 28th ranking. On the related tourism question, about the likelihood of a respondent visiting the country if money were no object, Israel was ranked bottom overall, 35th amongst Americans, and 32nd amongst Russians; and when we asked whether respondents believed that the people of the country would make them feel welcome if they visited, Israel again came bottom of the list, 29th amongst Americans and 32nd amongst Russians. If Israel's intention was, as Tzipi Livni said, to promote itself as a desirable place to live and invest in, the challenge appeared to be a steep one.

Israel would seem to be in a lonely position too, as far as public opinion goes. Despite the fact that official government policy towards Israel is supportive amongst its allies, public opinion in these countries is considerably less warm, and Israel ranks at or near the bottom of the index for all the European and North American panels. Palestine is not included in the NBI, but it seems likely that public opinion amongst its allies and supporters would more closely reflect the official position of their governments than is the case with Israel.

The country panel least positive about Israel in the NBI was Egypt, which ranked Israel 36th on every question in the survey apart from a 29th position on the question 'how strongly do you agree with the statement that this country makes a major contribution to innovation in science and technology' – the question on which Israel typically received its best marks (Russia gave Israel 12th position here).

But even a country like Germany, where views on Israel amongst the general population are likely to be more balanced, seldom ranked Israel above the bottom ten places in the survey. The highest ranking given to Israel by the German panel was a mere 23rd place on the question which asks whether respondents agree with the statement that 'this country has a rich cultural heritage', a ranking which is very much lower than the country objectively deserves. The political aspects of the country's image appeared to be contaminating perceptions of other areas of national interest which, in theory, should be entirely unrelated. However much one might disapprove of the policies of a country's government or even of successive governments, this shouldn't really have any impact on one's views of its natural landscape or its past cultural achievements. Yet the case of Israel shows that there is no absolutely impenetrable barrier between the world's perceptions of national politics and its perceptions of national culture, society, economics, history or even geography, and if the politics create sufficient disapproval, no area of national interest is safe from contamination. America should take note.

Israel appears to recognize the problem, and continues to be determined to do something about it. But the NBI and much other research confirm that national image is a phenomenon that changes very slowly if it changes at all. Sometimes, national image can take a severe knock from a catastrophic piece of behaviour: the Danish cartoons is a case in point, but the impact was by no means universal nor permanent, and after a time, people almost always seem to revert to their previous beliefs about countries. The only thing that can permanently change a country's image is a permanent change in the country and in the way it behaves.

Unfortunately for places like Israel, it is virtually impossible for a country to argue with public opinion. If Israel feels, as it clearly does, that it is misunderstood and misrepresented, simply repeating its own side of the argument is unlikely to achieve very much, no matter how creatively, loudly or persuasively it does so, and no matter how much it spends on media to reinforce the argument. Fighting negative perceptions with commercial communications techniques is akin to fighting terrorism with conventional weapons: no matter how vast the defence budget or how sophisticated the weaponry, the 'enemy' is simply too diffuse, too mobile and too committed for such measures to have any real effect.

Public opinion on such matters tends to be largely immovable except where it is very lightly held, and this is clearly not the case with Israel: as the NBI data confirms, people's views about Israel are notably passionate. Indeed, major publicity or propaganda campaigns like the one Israel seems to be contemplating are likely to be counter-productive in such circumstances: the more people suspect that a foreign power is trying to make them change their minds about something, the more firmly they will believe that it is attempting to deny or conceal the truth, and the more fiercely they will maintain their views.

The Israeli government's idea that improving people's understanding of its position and broadening knowledge of the non-military facets of their country will alter people's view of the country is a common one in such situations: 'to know us is to love us' is also a long-standing American fixation. The United States has already started to learn the lesson that for the populations which like America least, the opposite is true: the more they know about the USA, the *less* they like it, and the same may well be true for Israel.

Countries are judged by what they do, not by what they say; and as America discovered to its cost, when public opinion is strongly against a country, even its most praiseworthy and disinterested actions are likely to be ignored or interpreted in a negative light. Nothing less than a sustained and comprehensive change of political, social, economic and cultural direction will – ultimately – result in a changed reputation, so it is no surprise if most governments feel that unpopularity is the lesser cost of the two (some even find a grim sense of vindication in their very unpopularity).

It is also unsurprising that like the Israelis, so many governments are tempted against all logic, experience or common sense to pursue the chimerical third option of directly manipulating international public opinion. But it is clear that propaganda can only work well in closed and controlled societies, and in our massively interconnected, media-literate and healthily sceptical globalized world, it is a currency whose value has fallen virtually to zero.

Switzerland

It's odd, for a country that hosts so many important international sporting events and sporting bodies, that Switzerland's weakest area, in terms of its national image, should be sport.

Switzerland has come top of the list for **governance** ever since I started running the Nation Brands Index: if the world had to pick one government to rule the planet, Switzerland is the almost unanimous choice. It also scores very high for tourism, products, technology, ecology, and a host of other attributes, but comes in at 22nd place for sporting prowess.

Of course you could argue that it hardly matters: for a country with such a positive image, how serious can it really be that people don't think of the Swiss as top-rank sportsmen and women?

The problem is that sport isn't the only part of the **culture** dimension on the Nation Brand Hexagon where Switzerland scores poorly: there is a perception that the country has very little culture, either traditional or contemporary. And this is undoubtedly linked to the fact that Swiss people are admired and respected more than they are loved: like the Germans and the British, they appear to be the sort of people you'd willingly hire, but don't especially covet as friends. People want to be friends with the Italians, the Brazilians, the Canadians and especially the Australians, but not the Swiss. Perhaps it's that reputation for discretion and humourlessness, or perhaps it's simply that there is no convenient cliché to hand about what Swiss people are like, and so they remain largely anonymous in the world's imagination. In other words, Switzerland has a tremendously powerful *country* image, but a rather weak *national* image.

Given what I've said about how nations – such as Italy – can 'go out of fashion' as public opinion and general moral views and values evolve around them, this fact might put Switzerland and its enviably pristine image at risk. In fact, a quick look at Switzerland's NBI scores shows that it is declining almost as fast as Italy and the USA: nearly 2% during the last two and a half years. That may not sound much, but given that most country images are more like a fixed asset than a liquid currency, any steady decline, no matter how shallow, is a matter for concern.

Five or ten years ago, the qualities which many people seemed to admire in other countries were simple things like prosperity, modernity, attractive landscapes, economic growth, cool products. Today, what makes a positive national reputation has become more nuanced, and questions of integrity, generosity, environmental friendliness, transparency and democracy come into the equation more and more strongly.

In the absence of any clear idea of what the Swiss people have to offer in terms of their values, their personality or their philosophy of life, it is easy to see how the old clichés of cuckoo-clock Switzerland could turn against Switzerland's image. That famous Swiss-banker integrity and secrecy could start to look like corruption, especially at a moment when people are demanding more transparency in high finance; that famous wealth could look like selfishness; that famous precision could look like smugness; that famous competence could look like arrogance; that famous taste for producing and consuming the best of everything could look like smugness and élitism.

Faced with the huge challenge of introducing the Swiss to the world, sport is a singularly appropriate, powerful and eloquent 'language'. As Germany discovered when it hosted the football World Cup in 2007, the way a country hosts big sporting events and competes in them can be a highly effective way of communicating warmth and depth of national character; and the Sydney Olympics were no less important in helping to create the strong affection which people around the world feel for the Australians today.

If Switzerland learns to speak sport alongside its other 'languages' of culture, tourism, politics, foreign aid and exported products and services, it could do far more than merely fend off the danger of losing relevance in the coming decades.

Consider that if Switzerland's NBI ranking for culture were in the top 5 along with its other scores, Switzerland would now be challenging the UK and Germany for 'most admired nation' status.

Its people apart, Switzerland is one of those very few places whose identity is so powerful, so positive and so universally understood and admired, that the main task facing Swiss industry, Swiss institutions and the Swiss government is not how to improve or even maintain their national image, but to protect it against contamination from sub-standard products, firms from other countries claiming to be 'Swiss-made', companies using the Swiss flag without authority, and many other related threats. Only a few other places have this kind of reputational power: New York (you can put 'I ♥ New York' on a t-shirt and it's immediately worth more money), Amsterdam, London, Italy, France, and that's about it. Most other places on earth face a much harder task: how to earn that kind of profile in the first place.

There are a number of other countries out there whose natural national imagery is also well worth protecting, even if their national image isn't quite as perfect as Switzerland's. Jamaica is a prime example: for decades, the sounds of Reggae and the colours of Rasta and all the rest of that extraordinary country's rich national identity have been loved, admired, recognized around the world ... and then stolen. Jamaica has scarcely ever benefited economically from its national identity: the American and Spanish-owned resorts make most of the money from its tourism, the foreign sports shoe and clothing companies that decide when Rasta is cool make the money from its colours and images, the foreign record companies make the money from its music – and the extraordinary thing is that Jamaica keeps producing the culture without ever enjoying more than a small portion of its benefits.

As Switzerland figures out how to protect and manage its natural intellectual assets around the world, a host of countries like Jamaica might find that a very interesting case to study, and perhaps to emulate.

Latvia

Latvia faces a problem which is common throughout its neighbourhood: the urgent need to try and rebuild a national identity and reputation which the Soviet Union almost entirely erased.

This is one of the less recognized impacts of Soviet rule: by cutting off all movement of trade, culture, people and communications between its satellite states and the rest of the world, the Soviet system effectively destroyed the public identities of these countries. Now, they have to painstakingly rebuild those identities, brick by brick.

The lucky countries are the ones that were left with beautiful cities – like Riga, Prague, Ljubljana, Krakow and Budapest – as they have been able to attract plenty of tourists to their cities and thus re-open a dialogue with the West, and beyond: for the Ryanair generation, the appeal of such places has little to do with their past, and everything to do with their nightlife, their affordability and their cool. The countries and cities without obvious tourist appeal and without budget airline links have a far harder task ahead of them.

Spain, too, had an easier job 're-introducing' itself to Europe after the death of Francisco Franco, because his rule was short enough for Europeans still to share a common memory of Spain as a dynamic, modern European democracy. People only needed to be reminded of this, and to be reassured that Spain was once again open to the world and open for business, and Spain could pick up the pieces of its shattered reputation again. But few people outside Eastern and Central Europe have any conception of countries like Poland, Romania, Bulgaria, Hungary or the Baltic States as free countries with their own proud histories, cultures, personalities, products, landscapes, traditions, languages and people.

There are few bigger crimes than what was done in the name of Communism during the last century: entirely obliterating a country's good name and its history and identity, along with the centuries of its progress and cultural growth, and like some global game of snakes and ladders, sending it back to square one to fight for recognition in a busy, highly competitive, and largely indifferent world.

And speaking of board games, the US company Parker Games launched the Monopoly World Edition website last year, where people could vote for the cities that were to be featured in the new Global Edition of the game. The contest was announced in a Latvian newspaper, and Riga soon rose from 46th to 2nd position. Parker Games presumably then was faced with the dilemma of either assigning some of the most valuable real estate on the board to this virtually anonymous ex-Communist city, or else risking international opprobrium and overriding the popular vote: naturally, thousands of the good citizens of Riga had got voting, and succeeded in pushing their city way up the rankings. I say 'naturally', because almost nothing is more natural – or more powerful – than people's love of their own city, region or country.

Parker, I'm glad to report, did the honourable thing: Riga now sits proudly alongside Montréal on one of the two coveted dark blue squares on the board – and who knows? Perhaps a generation of children around the world are growing up with an unshakeable conviction in the back of their minds that Riga is one of the world's poshest cities.

A similar phenomenon was observed last year when the Swiss film-maker and adventurer Bernard Weber had the idea of creating a ranking for the 'New Seven Wonders of the World'. The event resulted in over one hundred million votes being cast around the world, as ordinary people voted frantically to get 'their' national landmark recognized as one of the new seven wonders. As I write in mid-2009, Weber's firm is launching a new initiative: the New Seven Wonders of the Natural World, and they are talking coolly of receiving *one billion* online votes.

It's striking because such events are somewhat unfamiliar. But if you think about it, equally dramatic displays of widespread and energetic patriotism are regularly triggered for every football World Cup, every Olympic Games, and to a lesser extent for contests such as 'Miss World'. Whenever people have an opportunity to boost the profile of their home town or home country, they do it, and in huge numbers. In the Eurovision Song Contest, where people can't vote for their own country, we see instead the utterly compelling spectacle of hundreds of thousands of people practising real-time public diplomacy, and voting for the countries they most wish to appease, flatter or flirt with.

Clearly, powerful forces are being unleashed here, and in a way it's reassuring to find that in our age of globalization such a simple and elemental instinct as patriotism is alive and well – and especially encouraging that it usually manages to find its outlet in harmless fun.

Such contests are undoubtedly 'good branding' for the places that do well in them: in one way or another, they will help to raise the profile of the place, increase tourism numbers, encourage other kinds of commercial interest such as foreign invesent and trade, and boost the number of people who decide to study, work and relocate there.

But all those millions of ordinary citizens certainly aren't voting for their home town because the tourist board has asked them to (most people are blissfully unaware that their city or country even has a tourist authority, and many even complain about the number of foreign visitors cluttering up their streets) or even because they necessarily see a direct connection between their vote and their future prosperity. It appears to be something purely instinctive, an almost automatic outpouring of group pride, and the expression of our own identity through the place that made us.

As I first reported in the 3rd Quarter Report of the 2005 Nation Brands Index, the way in which people rank the 'brand images' of their own countries follows a fascinating pattern. Every country in the overall Top 10 of the NBI ranks itself first, while every country in the bottom 30 rates one or more other countries higher than itself – with the exception of two of the fastest-growing economies in the world, India and Ireland. It's impossible to say whether this is cause or effect: do people rate their own country highly because they know how admired and admirable it is, or does the fact they rate it so highly help it to become admired and admirable?

The reality is that it's probably both at the same time, and there is some kind of feedback loop going on here. Ask 100 Chief Executives the secret of their company's strong brand, and half of them will probably tell you that it's the belief of their own staff in that brand and its values. Loyalty builds success, and success builds loyalty, and no place on earth – city, town, country, village or region – can hope to make others respect and admire it unless it first respects and admires itself.

But of course there's a catch. As with anything else that involves getting large numbers of people to make the effort to do something they don't normally do – even if it's only a matter of visiting a website and clicking on a button – there is a limit to how many times this force can be successfully unleashed. Yes, people undoubtedly do feel a strong pride in their own country or city, but their energy to express it is, like anything else, limited. You can't keep stoking the fire of patriotism forever: unless provided with new fuel, it will eventually die down and burn out.

Governments should reflect on this. Poking the embers of a population's love of their country will, nine times out of ten, produce a blaze, and this is a trick that any child can perform. But keeping the fire going for generations, without burning the house down, is a steeper challenge altogether.

America

When states are engaged in foreign policy directions which create widespread international ill-feeling, it is important that the population of the country is given an international voice, and permission to broadcast a different point of view. Otherwise, if the policies are deeply unpopular and prolonged, there is a risk that international disapproval can eventually contaminate other more precious (and innocent) aspects of national life. The Nation Brands Index suggested, for example, that disapproval of the American invasion of Iraq affected the world's view of the American population, American products, American culture and even the American landscape itself (people rate it as less beautiful than they did when I started running the survey in 2005).

In such times, it is important to remind the world of the distinction between State and Nation. The traditional view of governments is that in times of conflict, it is important to create a picture of domestic solidarity and support for foreign policy: in fact, it is probably wiser to do exactly the opposite, if the government truly has the long-term interests of the country at heart. The more a government allows and encourages dissenting voices to emerge from its own citizens, the more principled actions that are carried out – even or especially if they are politically opposed to the foreign policy – the more emphasis that is placed on cultural values, and so forth, the more effectively the national reputation is protected against the damaging effect of the government's overseas adventures. And this act of protection is essential, because a strong and positive national reputation is fundamental to doing business, attracting talent and capital and visitors, supporting the government's other international engagements, and eventually to recovering the esteem in which the nation is held once the foreign policy has run its course.

This does not mean that business, or culture, or society have to become apologists for their government's foreign policy: quite the contrary. They should be allowed to express dissent, encouraged to 'defend the honour of the population', and helped to speak more loudly about other aspects of national life. This is why, in the United States, the work of Business for Diplomatic Action is so important: by encouraging good commercial diplomacy amongst American businesses operating abroad, it is helping to protect the 'brand' of America against further damage, and ensuring a quicker recovery of the national reputation once the policy direction changes.

This argument suggests that in times of unpopular overseas engagements, it might be more productive for a government to invest heavily in areas such as tourism promotion, cultural relations and export promotion than in overtly political public diplomacy: dropping bombs out of one plane and leaflets out of the next is patently futile, and trying to persuade people to love you when they have good reason to hate you is likely to be counter-productive. You can't argue with public opinion, and it is very difficult to change the subject. But strong reminders of the reasons why perhaps people liked your country in the first place is likely to do less harm and might even do some good.

Philanthropy (when it's international in scope) is also important in shaping national image because it's one of the few ways in which the people of the country can 'speak' directly and unofficially to the rest of the world, and thereby remind us that we shouldn't deduce too much about the character and values of the whole nation from the policies of its government. The act of giving away large sums of private money can make news on its own account, and is thus a self-amplifying and self-promoting means of demonstrating that the values and morals of the population are still in good shape.

And, increasingly, sub-national actors such as states, regions and cities can, by acting on moral principles that differ from those of the national government, help to prove that it might make sense for people in other countries to be against the government, but not against the nation. Such players have the advantage that their images are not usually associated with any particular politics, and that they can 'do' international relations without being held responsible for foreign policy. California's more responsible stance on climate change during the second Bush presidency is a good example of this: and with the increasing political and economic power of cities, it is clear that city diplomacy is likely to play a significant role in international relations in the coming years.

There is, alas, no such thing as international democracy, and no matter how deeply people in other countries might be affected by the decisions of the US President, they have no say in his or her election – although during the election campaign of President Obama, it was pretty clear that many people in many other countries would have liked to have been able to cast their vote. In the absence of such mechanisms, it is all the more important that the people of the country, its businesses and culture, have the means to separate their 'civil' reputation from the 'statal' one which is both the responsibility and the dessert of their government.

National governments will find, even when they try to pursue the most ethical of foreign policies, that from time to time it is difficult to avoid making enemies. It is at such times that being able to call on different voices is the best insurance policy against longer term reputational damage. A prudent government will see the sense of investing constantly in longer-term cultural, commercial and social relations with other states, and building up a substantial international store of goodwill, respect and mutual understanding, at least partly in the expectation that such events will, sooner or later, probably occur.

The unpopularity of the USA around the World, and especially in countries with large Muslim populations, has been endlessly written and spoken about. Opinion ratings have slumped, particularly since the USA began its post-9/11 'War on Terror'.

But are opinion polls a good guide to brand strength? The evidence from the Nation Brands Index suggests that they may not be. Despite the misgivings most Muslim people have about the US Government and its behaviour in recent years, those in the four 'Muslim countries'[9] in the NBI still rank the USA as the strongest overall brand compared with any other of the World's major geo-political groupings (and this is on the basis of data collected while George W. Bush was still in office).

Table 5.1 presents the average ranking by the four 'Muslim countries' for ten geo-political groupings, including the USA, China, Russia and India. To increase the reliability of these results, we merged five quarters' results from the NBI in 2006 and 2007, thus reducing the margin of error[10] to under 1%.

The consensus in the four countries, taken together, is that USA has the strongest brand among these blocs. Five individual countries – Japan, UK, Germany, France an Italy – are ranked higher than the USA; but when all but the largest countries are placed in geo-political groups, the USA emerges as the strongest in the eyes of the Muslim group, as Table 5.1 shows.

Naturally, there are aspects of the USA's brand that are stronger than others. In fact, in the eyes of most people in the survey – not just Muslims – there are some that are very weak. Governance is, not unsurprisingly, a weak area, particularly the USA's contribution to international peace and security. USA was rated 23rd for Governance by the four 'Muslim' countries. Tourism was just as weak. One reason why Tourism was a weak dimension for the USA – and why the USA has been prevented from leading the Culture dimension – is that people rate it very low for heritage. This is a universal assessment, not only a Muslim one.

What is abundantly clear – and this is the essence of high-profile, complex brands like the USA's – is that these weak dimensions of

Table 5.1 How Muslims view the world

Rankings of major blocs by 4 'Muslim' countries	Average NBI^TM position
USA	6
Core EU	9
UK and the 'Old Commonwealth'	10
Southern Europe	12
China	13
East Asia (without China)	14
Russia	19
4 'Muslim' countries	22
India	27
Latin America	29

Figure 5.1   How four countries with majority Muslim
populations see the USA

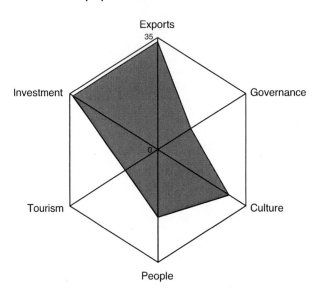

the brand have not had a serious dampening effect on the strong
dimensions, notably Exports and Invesent and Immigration. This
is also true of sub-dimension areas such as contemporary culture.
USA was 2nd in Exports and Invesent and Immigration, and in
contemporary culture despite many Muslims' misgivings about the
morality of Western popular culture.

Countries with lower profiles like Denmark, or with simpler brands
like Italy, are much more vulnerable if one or two of their key brand
dimensions are damaged. The collapse of Denmark's brand in Egypt,
following the cartoons controversy in early 2006, is an extreme case
of this. Denmark's scores in all six dimensions plummeted, and
in some cases have only partially recovered after nearly three years.
Despite what many Muslims regard as greater affronts to their
world, the USA's brand has not collapsed in any of the four 'Muslim
countries'.

On the contrary, the USA's stronger dimensions – and even the
brand as whole – are rewarded more by the four 'Muslim countries'
than by most other panel groupings, as Table 5.2 shows.

Table 5.2   How the world views America

USA's overall ranking by 5 major blocs	East Asia	4 'Muslim' countries	Russia	Latin America	Core EU
	5	6	12	15	15

The USA's brand is weakest in Latin America and the core EU countries of Germany, France, Netherlands and Belgium. It is strongest among the large Asian countries and blocs – including India and China.

The clear message in these results is that much of the Muslim world wants to engage with the USA in areas that matter in their daily lives.

Albania

Albania, just like America, finds itself battling against a negative image, its officials also asking 'why do they hate us?', and also complaining that the good stories just don't seem to be able to get out.

Albania is in many ways the typical case of a transition state whose reputation lags painfully behind the reality: since the end of Communism, the country has made notable social and economic progress, but this appears to have had almost no impact on popular perceptions of the country. The 'professional' audiences – such as investors, diplomats, tour operators, bankers and business people – are, of course, better informed about the place, and some of them are quite excited about Albania's prospects, but the general public is 20 years behind the curve. From the way most Europeans talk about Albania, you would think that King Zog was still on the throne.

Albania's problem is the fact that most people are far too busy worrying about their own countries and their own lives to give much thought to a country they know little about and will probably never visit, and they are unlikely to go to any trouble to update the shallow, convenient, prejudiced narrative they hold in their heads about such places. Modest progress, growing stability and sensible reforms don't make headlines and don't interest people who have no personal connection with the place. Evil tyrants, self-styled monarchs, repulsive regimes, shocking repression: these are the stories that make the media and become the common currency of a country's international image.

If I've learned one thing in the years I've been working in this field, it's the sad, simple fact that public opinion will never voluntarily 'trade down' from a juicy story to a boring one.

Meanwhile, back across the Atlantic, successive public diplomacy officials, with their energetic and well-meaning attempts to communicate how tolerant and benign the USA really is to publics that, largely, detest the place – and for, largely, very good reasons – were suffering from the same misapprehension as the Government of Albania: both thought that the good stories would kill the bad ones.

They were both wrong. Strong stories can only be killed by stronger ones.

Bilbao and Dubai

People often ask me whether commissioning a big, glamorous new building will 'brand' their city. The answer is that it depends why you're doing it, and how original the building really, objectively is. If the building is highly expressive of something clear and interesting that your city is telling the world about itself – like the Guggenheim Museum in Bilbao, the Sydney Opera House or the Kunsthaus in Graz – then it might be a very effective piece of 'branding' (although it will achieve nothing on its own – it has to be one well-chosen part of a very long-term series of substantial actions that make the story real). If, on the other hand, it's done for its own sake and there's no real long-term strategy behind it, it will add nothing to the city's overall image at all.

Most of the 'trophy buildings' built in places like Dubai aren't expressive of anything in particular: they are just very large glass and steel filing-cabinets which, if they communicate anything at all, are simply monuments to money, power, modernity, technology, and the desire to show off. You need a veritable forest of such buildings before they really mean anything – and even then the only meaning is how much money there is in your city.

'Make me a landmark building' is no kind of brief for an architect: but 'tell the world our story' might be. Buildings must say something about their city and the country, or they are just bricks and mortar. Or steel and glass.

Asia

The level of interest in the images and reputations of places continues to grow, and apparently nowhere faster than in Asia. More money is being spent on various kinds of 'reputation management' – some of it wisely, but much of it not – by Asian cities, countries and regions than anywhere else on earth. In the rush to stake a claim in the new global economic order, countries from Bhutan to Oman and from Kazakhstan to Korea are talking about their 'brands' and attempting to wield some kind of influence over them.

Many of these countries are simply trying to ensure that their international reputations keep pace with the rapid growth of their economic and political power. Others believe that their strongly negative reputations are undeserved, and obstruct their progress. Still others believe that if only they could have *some* kind of image, and escape their current anonymity, they would be able to participate more effectively in the global marketplace.

In Asia as in every other part of the world, one sees governments falling into the same traps when it comes to national image and reputation: the 'naïve fallacy' that national image can somehow be built, reversed or otherwise manipulated through marketing communications; and the confusion between 'destination branding', which is a kind of sophisticated tourism promotion, and 'nation branding', which is usually understood as the management of the country's overall reputation.

One of the most prominent cases in Asia is Malaysia's long-running tourism campaign, featuring the slogan 'Malaysia Truly

Asia', which is often (wrongly) cited as a classic case of successful nation branding. In fact, this is *destination* branding, carried out with the specific intention of increasing visitors to the country. It was never intended, nor could it really aspire, to impact directly on the world's overall perceptions of the country, although of course there are plenty of opportunities for *indirect* impacts on the country's 'brand image' – not least the simple fact that if more people visit the country and enjoy themselves, they are more likely to spread the word and create a positive 'vibe' about the place.

A more rigorous habit of distinguishing between *sectoral promotion* – such as tourism, exports and invesent promotion – and 'nation branding', is an urgent need amongst the community of scholars, commentators and practitioners within this field, in Asia as elsewhere.

The idea of place branding in Asia is commonly associated with tourism today, since many Asian countries are now discovering that a healthy economy depends on a broad spread of risk: the countries that have traditionally relied on exports for their foreign revenues, such as Japan and South Korea, are now urgently attempting to build their visitor numbers, while the countries whose economies – and images – have tended to focus on their appeal as a destination, such as Thailand and the Maldives, are equally keen to broaden their image to embrace foreign direct invesent, exports and other sectors. Image goes hand-in-hand with economic development: a country that is strongly associated with certain sectors will always trade at a premium in those sectors, whereas a country that is not will always trade at a discount.

India is often cited for the vigour and ambition of its image-enhancing activities. Long prominent in tourism promotion, the country has more recently started to branch out into more general national image enhancement, and has had some notable successes in lobbying high-level decision makers – for example at the Davos forum in 2007, when India almost 'stole the show' with its ubiquitous self-promotion.

Most of the big 'branding stories' of Asia are, however, associated with exports. The tale of how Japan built its economy and its image after 1945 is frequently cited as an export-led branding miracle, and several other countries – South Korea, Singapore, Malaysia, Taiwan and of course China itself – have quite deliberately set themselves the task of repeating the Japanese miracle. As all of these countries have discovered, this journey is a long one. To develop the capacity to produce world-class consumer goods, to distribute them worldwide, to market them and to build the customer service capability behind them that today's consumers demand, is a decades-long task; and even once the industries are built and the products selling well around the world, an enhanced national reputation is depressingly slow to follow. Countries like Korea and Taiwan are disappointed to discover that, despite the huge successes of several of their manufacturers in other countries, and the major contribution such exporters have made to their economies, they are still not yet widely associated as a powerful country of origin for such goods.

If 'nation branding' is still in its infancy in Asia, the sister field of public diplomacy is equally so. The literature of public diplomacy is poor in Asian examples, and not all Asian ministries of foreign affairs even recognize the existence of such a discipline: Japan is a notable exception, and China – alongside its highly visible expansion into consumer markets overseas and its ever increasing invesent in tourism promotion – has made major advances in cultural diplomacy through the expansion of its Confucius Institutes around the world. Yet the region is hardly short of countries that would amply reward some analysis of their situations through the lens of public diplomacy – the impact of the 'Borat' movie on Kazakhstan's image, the pariah status of Burma and North Korea, the way the relationship between Taiwan and the People's Republic of China is played out in the public sphere, and so forth.

China

China's international image continues to slide quite rapidly downhill: exactly the opposite of what China's leadership was hoping for in the buildup to the all-important Beijing Olympics. Almost all of the ground its image had gained during the highly disciplined and stage-managed Olympics, plus some international sympathy as a result of a bad earthquake, was virtually wiped out as a result of a bad poisoning episode from baby milk, and the botched attempt to cover it up. It remains to be seen whether China's still relatively strong economic growth, as other major economies falter, will help to achieve what such 'nation branding' initiatives have so far failed to do, and persuade the world that China is a country to be trusted, and admired.

Repeated episodes relating to dodgy products made in China further damage the image of the country, and, as long as they continue, will significantly slow down the process of taking the 'Made in China' brand from merely ubiquitous to actually trusted, and ultimately desired. I once predicted that within ten years' time, we would start to see American and European products being launched on the marketplace with fake Chinese-sounding names in an attempt to make them appear more desirable than their real country of origin would allow: but this goal – which, let us not forget, Japan managed to achieve in just a few decades – looks further off than ever.

The Chinese leadership is frantic to create a better 'soft power' image for China in its potential marketplaces around the world, and the huge invesent in Confucius Centres, the Beijing Olympics, the Shanghai Expo, its increasing aid donations in Africa, the more moderate and collaborative foreign policy in some areas, the acquisition of trusted Western brands by Chinese companies, are all part of this strategy. In a speech to the 17th Party Congress, President Hu Jintao spoke again of his aim to create trusted Chinese export brands – echoing the same promise made several years ago by the then Vice-Premier Wu Bangguo, as I reported in my 2003 book *Brand New Justice* – but this ambitious and complex manoeuvre is proving exceedingly hard to stage-manage on China's own terms.

Part of the problem is that China is a bull in the global china shop, and is becoming simply too powerful to be able to carry out the delicate manipulations necessary to build a positive and trusted image in other countries. Take the news in late 2008 that the Chinese oil firm PetroChina trumped US rival Exxon Mobil to become the world's biggest firm, with a market capitalization of a trillion dollars: no matter how you tell a story like this, the reaction of many ordinary people is more likely to be fear than liking or respect.

Brand China is going from invisible to overbearing in one leap. At least the United States enjoyed a couple of centuries of admiration and affection before starting to experience the downside of its success in the global marketplace.

As I pointed out in *Brand America*, America's image problems have at least as much to do with its achievement of many of its economic aims as its frequently unpopular foreign policy: the world loves and supports a challenger, but let it succeed in its challenge and acquire the power it seeks, and the love will quickly turn to fear, and the fear to hatred. China is getting there in one short step.

China has the economic and increasingly the political strength to do pretty much whatever it wants: but the one thing it cannot do with all that power is to make itself much liked. And as its leadership has clearly understood, being liked is the fundamental prerequisite for building modern, market-based Empires on the U.S. model.

The results from the Nation Brands Index do not make comfortable reading for China. If we compare the NBI results for the 35 countries in the survey over the period between its first appearance in the Index in early 2005 and 2007, China experienced the worst trend of any country measured in the survey. Its overall score declined during this period by 4%. This may not seem much, but it is nearly double the ground lost by any other country in the NBI – and around 6% below the fastest improving countries like the Czech Republic and Brazil.

What is worse for China is that the decline is much greater than average in areas where it most needs traction in the international economic arena. The worst figures are in the Immigration and Invesent dimension and in particular for people's willingness to live and work in China – the 'talent magnet' question. For Immigration and Invesent as a whole, China's score declined by 11.4% between the final quarter of 2005 and the second quarter of 2007. For willingness to live and work in China, the figure was nearly 14%. This compares with drops of around 9% for Russia and Indonesia, the countries with the next most negative trends in this area. Only Israel is now less popular than China as a place to live and work.

China's bad news is not confined to the Immigration and Invesent dimension; for the country of origin effect on product purchase, the results were not good. If people find out that a product is made in China, the majority of people in the survey said they would be less inclined to buy it. What's more, the people who said they had bought products from China were even more negative than the respondents as a whole.

The trend for China's products was also the worst of any of the 35 countries. In the 2008 study, China is now 47th (the third lowest country) for products, compared with 24th in late 2005. Its score declined by nearly 6% over the '05–'07 period, compared for example with an increase of nearly 6% for Brazil, another of the quartet of largest emerging markets.

If China is hoping to emulate or even outstrip Japan's remarkable 40-year rise as a leading global producer of trusted and desirable consumer products, it appears to have taken a wrong turn in the road. The first stage of this process – familiarity with the 'Made in China' label through wide distribution of its products – has been achieved with remarkable speed and efficiency, but the second stage – where familiarity turns to trust – looks considerably more elusive. China's current highly publicized quality issues have certainly delayed this stage. The final stage – where trust turns to desire and premium positioning – can only take place when the corporations as well as the products are truly world-class, and can design and brand to world class standards, and this stage looks to be decades away for the majority of Chinese products. There are exceptions – Haier and Lenovo being perhaps the most high-profile examples – and of course there is always the option of 'fast-tracking' the process through the acquisition of already trusted foreign brands, an approach which both China and India see as part of their strategy.

China's tourism appeal is lagging too. People are showing no increase in their desire to visit China, despite the undoubted fascination of its historical heritage. In fact the trend in China's results for 'likely to visit, money no object' is the worst of any country – a drop of 5.6% since late 2005. China is now down in 21st position in the tourism brand rank, according to the 2008 study.

None of this augurs well for China and its attempts to promote itself as an attractive and trusted member of the international community. China's recent growth may have been stellar, but sooner or later it will have to base its economy on the sound footing of a comprehensive, robust and improving national reputation.

This must include a governmental system that people trust. How far people's perceptions of China's governance spill over into these other areas, we cannot say for sure. China showed one of the worst results for governance in the 2008 survey, outranking only Nigeria and Iran, and this included its results for competence in domestic governance. It is highly likely that if people have little confidence in a country's ability to manage itself, they will not be willing to invest their time and money in it, and a successful Olympic Games will certainly not have been sufficient to achieve the image turnaround they are hoping for.

Building a reputation, as China will discover, often feels like taking two steps forward and one step back: no sooner have you achieved something that makes people feel good about you, than it's forgotten. Governments must plan for the long term, and obsessively ask: 'what can we do next?' A successful Olympics is the start of the process, not the end; and of course it takes more than sporting events to build a national image: policy, products, people, culture, tourism and business have to work together to *earn* the country a better reputation. Only real changes, sustained over the very long term, can turn around a national image – especially one as bad as China's.

Yet it's not an impossible task: Japan and Germany both suffered from worse images than China's half a century ago, and are now amongst the most admired nations on earth. If any country has the patience and the resources to imitate those examples, it is surely China.

China, like India and indeed many countries in Asia, have for many centuries held a strong fascination over the imaginations of people in the West, and this glamour is an important component of their 'brand equity' in the age of globalization. But exoticism is a double-edged sword, and whilst such an image may support the tourism industry to a degree, and perhaps certain export sectors

– Chinese tea, Indian perfume, Japanese fashion – it can prove rather unhelpful for a country that is trying to build its reputation in financial services, engineering or technology. India's image is currently straddling these two sides of its image in a way which at times seems almost uncomfortable: a fundamental component of its tourism and cultural image, for example, is its poverty, and yet its more modern commercial image is an image of wealth. By the same token, the 'destination brand' of India is an image of chaos, almost of anarchy – hardly a useful attribute when one is trying to build a service economy based on efficient customer service or reliable motor vehicles.

This is, without question, an interesting stage in the maturity of the West's perception of the East. The facile and comforting clichés of 'the mysterious Orient' are the legacy of a less connected, less tolerant and more ignorant age, where engagement with other civilizations was limited to imperial adventures rather than true collaboration in a global marketplace. The de-mystification of the Orient is a necessary phase in human development, which implies major shifts in the reputational capital of the world.

Very few countries, in fact, have images that remain entirely consistent between East and West. South Korea is a classic case of a country that enjoys a rather positive reputation in its own 'neighbourhood' – the 'Korean wave' of commercial entertainment has made Korea something of a celebrity in East and even South Asia, but the wave doesn't reach Europe or the Americas, where – at least according to the Nation Brands Index – there appears to be substantial confusion between South Korea and its northern neighbour (to the obvious disadvantage of the South).

Most of the 'Asian Tiger' economies of East Asia are generally admired in Europe, yet there is a strong prejudice against them amongst South American populations, and especially in Brazil. The Brazilians show a remarkable distaste for most Far Eastern countries which is entirely out of kilter with 'global' views. One can only surmise what this antipathy stems from, but it does suggest that the world is still very far from united in a common sense of national reputation and image.

Democracy and place image do not always go easily or simply together, and it is noticeable that two of the places most widely recognized for the grip they have managed to exert over their international reputations – Dubai and Singapore – are both places that are run on somewhat corporate lines. This is surely no accident: the main reason why building a brand in the corporate sector is so much more straightforward than doing the same for a place is precisely because corporations have a supreme commander in the shape of their CEO, whose vision tends to form the defining narrative of the place, and deviation from this narrative often results in dismissal. Whatever one might say about North Korea, one has to admit that its brand is clear, simple and consistent – again, the consequence of the entire society being run along the lines of one man's viewpoint.

It remains to be seen whether India, the world's largest democracy, or China, the world's fastest-developing economy and the last major bastion of Communism, will eventually prove more successful at managing their reputations in the eyes of the world. So far, it looks very much as if democracy is winning the day, but the determination, resources and skill of the Chinese should never be underestimated.

CHAPTER 6

When Does Marketing Make Sense?

I have made the point that the effectiveness of commercial marketing communications – such as advertising and graphic design – is really only proven when a product or service is on sale to a specific target group, but there are other situations when such approaches are viable.

For instance, there have been cases of highly effective public service campaigns in many countries: advertising that has worked marvels in persuading people to wear seatbelts, quit smoking, avoid drink driving, donate to charities or show consideration to minorities. There have also been many campaigns that have persuaded people to join the armed forces, or vote for a particular candidate or political party. And there have been many 'branding' campaigns designed purely to enhance the image of a corporation, rather than to sell its products or services.

It seems that a precondition for the effectiveness of any advertising message is that the audience are prepared to 'give permission' for the sender to address them with this kind of message: the act of communication must be perceived as legitimate. This legitimacy isn't by itself a sufficient condition for the campaign to be effective, but I would suggest that it is a necessary one. Once legitimacy is established, then the effectiveness of the campaign is more of a technical matter, and depends on many complex factors: the preparedness of the audience to change its mind or behaviour; the quality, appeal and cogency of the messaging; delivery of the message at the appropriate frequency in the appropriate media; and so forth.

In other words, first you have to be allowed to speak, and people have to be prepared to listen to you; only then do you have an opportunity to persuade them to change their minds.

I would argue that whilst many other kinds of non-selling campaigns have proved effective, none of them are really analogous to campaigns designed to 'brand' countries, regions or cities, because they all pass the fundamental test of legitimacy, while messages from foreign governments seeking the approval or admiration of nationals in other countries do not.

Public service campaigns are usually targeted at the general public by their own governments, and explicitly so – strictly speaking, it may be propaganda, but at least it's 'white' propaganda (the kind where the true source of the message is acknowledged). Because the message is one which reinforces a strong cultural, moral or social value which most people already accept, the content is usually non-controversial (even if the treatment may need to be shocking to be effective). Few people would argue that smoking or drink-driving are harmful, or that it's good to wear a seatbelt or give money to starving people. For all these reasons, the audience effectively 'grants permission' to the government or other body to transmit this message. Then, if the point is well made, a changed attitude or behaviour may follow.

Recruitment campaigns, whether for the armed forces or for other companies or institutions, are perceived as legitimate because something is on offer, and a deal is being proposed. The audience then has a clear opportunity to evaluate the offer being made, and decide whether to respond to the advertisement. In effect, this is a selling situation: the product on offer is a career (or at least a job interview), and the payment requested is the target's labour (or at least their application).

Political campaigns are perceived as legitimate, at least in democratic societies, because the basic principle is accepted that parties and candidates need to be able to 'show their wares' to voters, so that voters can decide which way to vote. The political ad is also very much like selling a product: the product on sale is the manifesto or regime being offered, and the price being asked is the target's vote.

'Branding' campaigns for corporations or other institutions are harder to categorize (and their effectiveness is, by definition, hard to measure). Very often, they have a somewhat hidden agenda – for

example, raising the profile of an unknown corporation behind a well-known brand prior to a share offering, boosting the morale of the corporation's staff, reassuring shareholders that the corporation is solid and serious, preparing the public for a change of name – a 'rebranding' exercise – or announcing a merger. In several of these cases, the legitimacy of the transaction is provided by the fact that the advertisement is an announcement, and thus presumably of benefit to its target audience.

However, pure 'branding' campaigns, which are simply designed to make people feel good about a particular company, or to establish its style or character or values in the mind of the public, are probably rather less cost-effective. With no announcement to make and no product to sell, it is likely that they are ignored by the majority of people who are exposed to them: if an ad isn't asking you to do anything, offering you anything you want, or telling you anything you need or want to know, it is likely that you will screen it out.

If the campaign is exceptionally beautiful, funny, moving, thought-provoking, controversial, weird or otherwise captivating to watch (and this is most likely to happen with TV or cinema advertising as it's very difficult to captivate an indifferent consumer without sound and moving images), and screened sufficiently often, it may itself 'become the product' and make people talk about it. However, whether this then translates into any kind of changed behaviour or changed attitude will depend entirely on whether it is quickly followed up with a 'call to action' of some sort: a real message, a real offer, or a real product that can be clearly recognized as coming from the same source as the original campaign. If not, the memory of the campaign will fade away very quickly. Thus, the 'branding campaign' is really only a 'teaser campaign' for a more concrete and traditional transaction – a means of 'softening up' or preparing the audience for the offer which is to follow.

Most 'nation branding' campaigns carried out by governments in an attempt to raise the profile, improve the standing, enhance knowledge about or generate admiration for their country by foreign audiences are broadly modelled on these kinds of corporate branding campaigns. However, since they are seldom if ever followed up by any kind of 'call to action' – and arguably can't be, because nothing is required of the audience except a change of attitude – it is likely that any emotional effect or interest they may create on the audience, if they are sufficiently striking and well produced, will quickly fade away.

The other problem with such advertising is that it never really talks about anything except itself. Without anything in particular to offer the consumer, nor any possibility of showing much empathy with or knowledge of the consumer, the sum of the message, however elegantly couched, is really nothing more than 'we think our country is wonderful'. To such a message, the most likely response is 'well you would, wouldn't you?'

Whether or not such campaigns are considered to have any legitimacy with the audience needs further research, but the reality is that they are very, very seldom striking enough, well enough produced, believable yet original enough, to 'become the product' in the way that a successful corporate branding campaign needs to do if it has any chance of success.

Most 'nation branding' films I've seen are simply strings of library shots of the country's most impressive buildings, beaches and landscapes, interspersed with shots of smiling families, aeroplanes taking off (look! we have airports!), chemists in white coats looking at blue fluids in glass beakers (look! we do science!), and trails of red tail-lights stretching along night-time freeways (look! we have cars!), set to pompous and triumphal music tracks with just a hint of something ethnic, in order to create the correct impression of respect for ancient traditions co-existing with a dynamic and thrusting modernity. It is remarkable what a great job these films do of making very different countries look virtually identical, and it's hard to believe that they achieve anything else at all, except of course for enabling the department that commissions them to prove that it has actually spent its promotional budget and not handed it out to friends and family.

Most 'nation branding' exercises, however, don't even aspire to the potentially powerful emotional effects of film, but are limited to static graphic design, slogans and 'brand strategies'. In other words, rather than attempting to mimic the high-profile branding campaigns of corporations, most countries seem to stop short at corporate identity, a much more modest exercise which is merely designed to ensure that the 'look and feel' of a company's printed and manufactured materials, buildings, uniforms and vehicles are consistent. The idea is that anybody who encounters the company in any setting will 'get the same message'. A great deal of research and creative thinking goes into ensuring that the true spirit and essence of the company's values, mission and personality are fully reflected in the graphic device, in the colours and typefaces chosen, and are perfectly summarized in the corporate slogan.

All of this makes reasonably good sense for companies that are operating in a busy commercial environment. Building a solid and positive reputation has quite a lot to do with consistency, and a company that looks like itself inside and out will find it easier to create positive feelings amongst its staff, suppliers, shareholders and customers. It's exactly the same principle with uniforms for armies.

But whether any of this makes sense for a country is quite another matter. Is it really possible, or desirable, to sum up the 'essence' of an entire nation in a series of coloured squiggles? Can it really embrace such very different offerings as tourism (which usually emphasizes the idyllic past of the country to a mass audience) and foreign investment promotion (which usually emphasizes the technological future of the country to an elite audience) without being reduced to something absurdly bland and unmemorable? Can the history, culture, politics, landscapes and endeavours of an entire population really be summarized in a few monosyllables in the English language? Will this really ensure that the 'staff' (i.e. the population) of the 'corporation' (i.e. the country) and their 'consumers' (i.e. the remainder of the world's population) are always presented with a clear, consistent and compelling synthesis of the country's values and mission? Will it really serve to distinguish the 'brand' (i.e. the country) from its 'competitors' (i.e. every other country on the planet), and does it need to? Will it really create a 'sense of mission' in government, business and the general population? Will it really make anyone change their minds about a country they've hardly heard of, or about which they have believed pretty much the same things for most of their lives?

It seems unlikely.

Tourism, by contrast, is a refreshingly simple and honest business. The main purpose of a tourist board is selling a more or less tangible product – a holiday – to a consumer who is in the market for such a product; so, unlike many other branches of national endeavour, the relevance of its messages to the foreign audience is beyond doubt. As long as the tourist board has enough marketing expertise, resources and patience, it can be fairly sure of increasing tourism arrivals.

Tourism is worth mentioning in this context, however, because it has a secondary impact which is less well recognized, and which in fact makes it one of the few means by which the overall 'brand image' of a country *can* in fact be enhanced.

A happy holiday experience self-evidently has the power to change the 'brand image' of that country, quickly and forever, in the mind of the holidaymaker. People frequently abandon their preconceptions about countries once they visit them: at least for those individuals, the country stops being a brand and becomes a real country. Indeed there is some evidence from the NBI to show that preference for a country and its people, politics, culture and products tends to increase as a result of *any* personal experience of that country, even when the holiday experience is not positive.

This factor is significant, because people talk to other people about their holidays. If enough people visit the country, especially if they are part of an influential demographic, then over time this can create a real and quite possibly measurable improvement in the country's overall international image. And of course it's a virtuous circle: the better the image, the more people will want to visit the country.

So it follows that destination marketing, in addition to its primary purpose of encouraging visits, can play an important secondary role in helping visitors to form a compelling personal narrative about the country, which enhances their power as 'viral agents' or informal advocates for the country's brand once they return home.

For this and for many other reasons, the integration of tourism and tourism promotion into the overall nation brand strategy is to be encouraged: but this integration brings two key challenges.

The first is one of balanced representation of the country. Tourism is frequently the loudest voice in communicating the country; the tourism sector often has the biggest marketing budgets and the most experienced marketers of any sector. This can, over many years, have the effect of drowning out the economic, political, industrial and even cultural voices, and creates a skewed, soft, leisure-oriented nation 'brand' which can easily conflict with a country's reputation as an exporter of quality products, a serious political player, a technological power, or a suitable destination for investment.

Britain, for example, has often suffered from a disconnect between the heritage Britain of the tourism narrative and the professional Britain of industry, commerce, politics and higher education. However, this dichotomy is today better managed than by many of Britain's competitors – and I would argue that the tourism narrative always benefits from the influence of the 'professional' narrative since it helps steer the destination marketing away from predictable 'me-too' heritage promotion, and towards the more interesting and engaging sphere of people, rather than empty landscapes.

The second challenge relates to the country's regional 'sub-brands'. The devolution of power and resources to regions is a powerful tendency in modern politics, especially when those regions have distinct cultural identities that demand the right to self-determination and self-expression. In political and social terms, the devolution agenda is hard to criticize, but from the point of view of national competitive advantage it can be highly counterproductive. The essence of social justice is diversity, but the essence of good marketing is simplicity, and this tension is seldom fully resolved.

When dealing with markets for tourism, investment and exports, the question of whether to represent and promote the nation as a single entity or as a series of 'sub-brands' really depends on the audience's familiarity with that nation. If, for example, one is marketing UK tourism to Americans, there is a strong argument for more 'specialized' marketing of regions, cities, counties and even towns: in order to keep regular customers interested, the offer needs to become ever richer and more detailed. If, on the other hand, one is competing for tourists in a market where there is little knowledge of one's country – such as marketing Britain in China, India, Russia or Brazil, for example – then the argument for 'branding Britain' is stronger. When the customer is unable to distinguish reliably between, say, England and Ireland, it is clearly not the time or place to be marketing the Cornish Riviera or Nottingham. As a general rule, if 'sub-branding' is likely to appeal to an expert audience, it is worth doing; if it is more likely to create confusion, it should be avoided, and regional resources should be pooled into supporting the national 'master brand'.

In the end, countries like Britain need to adopt what I call a 'box of chocolates' brand architecture. The brand on the outside of the box is 'Britain', and when familiarity is low, we should market the box. When familiarity is higher, we can open the box and introduce the individual chocolates: each one is distinctive, with its own flavours and appearances, but bearing a strong family resemblance and a clear connection to each other and to the brand on the box.

For the travel and tourism industry, these questions of national image are fundamentally important. The tourism industry contributes in a critical way to the formation and maintenance of the national image; but, by the same token, it depends on that image to a high degree.

The tourist board needs to 'sell the country' to a vast international audience of ordinary consumers as well as a highly informed professional cadre of tour operators and other influencers, and the background reputation of the country ultimately determines whether that 'selling' process is easy or difficult, expensive or cheap, simple or complex – and whether it gets gradually easier and more efficient over time, or whether it remains forever a struggle. A country's reputation determines whether its messages are welcomed, and whether they are believed.

This is the reason why the concept of destination branding has become so important. The idea of *brand equity* sums up the idea that if a place, product or service acquires a positive, powerful and solid reputation, this becomes an asset of enormous value

– probably more valuable, in fact, than all its tangible assets, because it represents the ability of the place or organization to continue to trade at a healthy margin for as long as its brand image stays intact. Brand equity also represents the 'permission' given by a loyal consumer base for the company or country to continue producing and developing its product range, innovating, communicating and selling to them.

Put simply, a destination with a powerful and positive image needs to do less work and spend less money on promoting itself to the marketplace, because the marketplace already believes what it is telling them. It merely has to help buyers find and purchase the product.

But destinations with powerful brands have a different task, one that destinations with weak brands don't have. Just like any respected corporation, a highly regarded place has a big responsibility to ensure that the reality always lives up to its reputation. Indeed, in order to protect itself against competitors, such a place must *exceed* expectations through constant innovation. This task can of course be just as costly and just as challenging as building a reputation in the first place, but having a good reputation does at least provide a steady flow of revenue to fund this work on the 'product' itself; so at one level, brand equity is as much about cashflow as anything else.

The idea of destination branding is important because it takes into account these important questions relating to the deliberate *capture* and *accumulation* of reputational value. Ordinary tourism promotion, when it's carried out with no particular long-term national strategy in mind apart from growth, is an endless cycle which may or may not lead to real progress in the longer term.

Unlike brand management, it's mainly about selling. It can certainly be effective at doing this, but unless the selling is directed and driven by an underlying brand strategy, there is little chance that the country as a whole will acquire any substantial brand equity, and so the promotional task never gets any easier or cheaper, and there is little chance that a price premium will ever be justified in the eyes of the consumer. The basic principle of destination branding is that every act of promotion, exchange or representation needs to be seen not as an end in itself but as an opportunity to build the country's image and reputation.

Clearly, marketing makes good sense when it comes to selling the nation's products, whether these are tourism offerings or other export products and services; and there is no doubt that well marketed tourism and export sectors can provide huge benefits to the nation's overall profile.

As I argued in *Competitive Identity*, the use of mass-marketing techniques for promoting foreign investment is less easily justifiable, since one is selling to a relatively small and well-defined audience of elite purchasers: in other words, it's a business-to-business nego-tiation, not a consumer sale, and in such circumstances, sales is probably a more relevant technique than marketing.

But when it comes to promoting the image of the nation itself, the government's policies, its culture or its people, the value and the appropriateness of traditional marketing communications techniques remain very much in doubt.

CHAPTER 7

Public Diplomacy and Place Branding: Where's the Link?

In March 2007, a conference on Public Diplomacy was held at Wilton Park, the conference centre of the United Kingdom's Foreign and Commonwealth Office. Public Diplomacy practitioners and academics from several different countries attended the event, and a lively discussion emerged around the future of PD. One strand of the debate that particularly interested me centred on the connection between PD and competitive identity.

Delegates sought to understand whether these were simply two versions of the same idea, one seen from an international relations perspective and the other from a more commercial angle, or whether they were in fact entirely different concepts; and if different, to what extent were they linked or compatible. The view I expressed to the conference was that Public Diplomacy is in fact a subset of competitive identity: I have always intended competitive identity to consider how the nation *as a whole* presents and represents itself to other nations, whereas PD appears to concentrate exclusively on the presentation and representation of *government policy* to other publics: in other words, the international equivalent of what is usually known as Public Affairs, or a type of diplomacy where the interlocutor is society at large rather than other diplomats or ministers.

According to the theory of competitive identity which I set out in my book of the same name, government policy is simply one point of the 'hexagon' of national image, one sixth of the picture which nations habitually paint of themselves, whether by accident or by design. From this point of view, PD is clearly a component of competitive identity: it is concerned with presenting one aspect of national activity, while competitive identity attempts to harmonize policy, people, sport and culture, products, tourism, trade and investment promotion and talent recruitment.

During the two years since that conference, my views on this matter have changed. My contention then that PD is a subset of competitive identity was, I realize, based on a rather conventional interpretation of Public Diplomacy as a *means of presentation and representation* of the national interest: in other words, that it was primarily concerned with the communication of policies rather than with their execution or conception. This seems to be doing the discipline a disservice, even if there are as yet few examples of PD rising above its conventional role of press and public affairs agency to the Ministry of Foreign Affairs: potentially, Public Diplomacy is the 'master discipline' of international relations for developed and prominent countries just as competitive identity is potentially the 'master discipline' of economic development for emerging and less well-known countries.

Ironically, my initially rather narrow view of PD was precisely analogous to the interpretation of competitive identity against which I have been battling for the last ten years: the idea that brand management for a nation (or city, or region) is simply a matter of marketing or promoting the place. During this period I have advanced many arguments for why this is often neither wise, effective nor even possible, and that the huge expenditures by governments on national promotional campaigns are, more often than not, a waste of taxpayers' or donors' money. Most publics today, I have always maintained, are simply too well inoculated against advertising and too savvy about the media to believe mere government propaganda.

Similar arguments have often been levied against conventional public diplomacy by its wiser practitioners. When Edward R Murrow, the 'father' of American PD and head of the United States Information Agency (USIA) found out about the CIA's botched attempt to invade Cuba at the Bay of Pigs in April 1961, he was 'spitting mad,' as the then Voice of America director, Henry Loomis, recalls. 'They expect us to be in on the crash landings,' Murrow said to Loomis. 'We had better be in on the takeoffs [too].'

President Kennedy apparently took this advice, for in January 1963 his administration issued the USIA new orders. Its role would no longer be merely to inform and explain U.S. objectives; it would be 'to help achieve United States foreign policy objectives by... influencing public attitudes in other nations.' This explicitly shifted the mission from information provision to persuasion, and from commentator (or apologist) to actor. The USIA would also have responsibility for 'advising the President, his representatives abroad, and the various departments and agencies on the implications of foreign opinion for present and contemplated United States policies, programs and official statements.'

The debate continues to this day, and Karen Hughes, the Under-Secretary for Public Diplomacy under George W Bush, frequently stressed that her job should not be limited to the communication of government policy: 'being in at the takeoffs' meant having an influence over the formation of those policies too. Her close relationship with President George W Bush was taken as an encouraging sign by the PD community that her department now stood a real chance of achieving its aims, since it was in a better position to have some influence over the way the 'takeoffs' were planned. These hopes, as it turned out, were not to be realized.

However, the main challenge to the work of Ms Hughes and her successors may not, after all, have much to do with their closeness to the President or the influence they wield over U.S. foreign policy: in the end, it is more likely to be the image, credibility and reputation of the country whose policies they seek to justify. The best under-secretary for public diplomacy is, in the end, the President, since he has the most influence over how the country behaves in the world; the best kind of public diplomacy for the United States is a foreign policy that is as moral as possible. But there is an element of *realpolitik* in the continued existence of this role and this department: it indicates an underlying assumption that his policies will forever be unpopular with somebody somewhere, and that therefore a 'secretary for apologies' will always be needed to clear up the mess afterwards.

If the purpose of public diplomacy is simply to promote or attempt to excuse government policies, it is likely to be superfluous or futile, depending on the good name of the country and its government at that particular time. If the country is generally in favour, then unless the policy is patently wrong-headed, it is likely to be well received by publics and simply needs to be clearly communicated. Relatively little art or skill are required to do this. If on the other hand the country suffers from a poor or weak reputation, especially in the area relating to the policy, then almost no amount of promotional skill or expenditure can cause that policy to be received with enthusiasm, and it will either be ignored or taken as further proof of whatever evil is currently ascribed to the country.

Clearly, the reputation of a country's current government may be held in higher or lower esteem than the underlying 'brand image' of the nation as a whole, and this is an additional complicating factor for governments attempting to understand how best to manage their international dialogue. When the nation has a better 'brand' than its government (a situation which is much more common than the converse), unpopular government policies may do little harm to the country's overall longer-term interests, but it is likely that an internationally unpopular government may over a long period cause damage to the 'nation brand' which is very difficult to undo, as I argued in my book *Brand America*.[11]

The complexity of understanding and managing public rather than professional opinion points to one of the key differences between traditional diplomacy and public diplomacy. When the target is a restricted and professional audience such as diplomats and ministers, the background reputation of the country in question, whilst it undoubtedly does play a role in conditioning those individuals' responses to its policies, has only a limited and indirect impact on the way in which they evaluate them. Such professional audiences are more likely to consider policies on their own merits, in detail, and to some degree in isolation of previous policies from the same country or even government.

It is, in fact, one of the principles of diplomacy that the fairest, most informed and most balanced view possible are always taken of any government's actions and their presumed motivations. Diplomats are, or should be, fully prepared to *change their minds* about any country at any point.

Publics, on the other hand, have neither the expertise, the experience, the habit or the desire to consider the actions of foreign governments so carefully and in so even-handed a manner, and their responses to those governments' policies are likely to be directly and substantially conditioned by their perceptions of the country as a whole. As I have mentioned, it is a common tendency of publics to hold on very tightly to a rather simplistic view of countries once it is formed (especially when considering more distant countries or those with which they have no particular connection), so public perceptions of countries tend to be very stable. The views of publics are therefore easier to measure and understand, but much harder to alter, whereas the views of governments and their foreign services may be harder to measure and understand, but at least in theory are more susceptible to alteration.

The comparison is analogous to the different ways in which a judge and a jury consider the prisoner in the dock: the trained legal mind will concentrate primarily on the supposed offence and on the evidence, whereas the public will tend to concentrate on the accused, the victim, and on their presumed characters, and may easily be led astray by circumstantial evidence. For this reason considerable thought is given in most democratic countries to *artificial* ways of preventing the jury from taking previous offences into consideration when reaching their verdict. In the court of international public opinion, of course, there can be no such provisions, and governments are thus largely at the mercy of their international reputation, and to a great extent the passive beneficiaries or victims of generations of their predecessors' wisdom or foolishness.

As I described in *Competitive Identity,* wise people have always understood that people's perceptions of the messenger can be more important than the message itself. The English novelist Anthony Trollope makes exactly the same point in his 1881 novel, *Dr Wortle's School*:

> *So much in this world depends on character that attention has to be paid to bad character even when it is not deserved. In dealing with men and women, we have to consider what they believe, as well as what we believe ourselves. The utility of a sermon depends much on*

the idea that the audience has of the piety of the man who preaches it. Though the words of God should never have come with greater power from the mouth of man, they will come in vain if they be uttered by one who is known as a breaker of the Commandments; – they will come in vain from the mouth of one who is even suspected to be so.

For this reason, Public Diplomacy is an emasculated discipline unless it has some power to affect the background reputation of the country whose policies it attempts to represent; and since that background reputation can only be significantly altered by policies, not by communications, the critical success factor for public diplomacy is whether its connection to policy making is one-way or two-way. If there is a two-way mechanism that allows the public diplomacy function to pass back recommendations for policy making, and these recommendations are taken seriously and properly valued by government as critical 'market feedback', then public diplomacy has a chance of enhancing the good name of the country, thus ensuring that future policy decisions are received in a more favourable light. It's a virtuous circle, because of course under these circumstances the policies need far less 'selling'.

Simply ensuring that the public diplomacy function has an influence over government policies, however, can only have a limited and delayed impact on the background reputation of countries. According to my theory of competitive identity, it is only when public diplomacy is carried out in coordination with the full complement of national stakeholders as well as the main policy makers, and all are linked through effective brand management to a single, long-term national strategy, that the country has a real chance of affecting its image and making it into a competitive asset rather than an impediment or a liability.

National governments are simply not in control of all of the forces that shape their country's image, and neither is any other single body within the nation. The tourist board cannot control government policies, yet those policies can dramatically affect its business; the success of the investment promotion agency may be influenced by the communications of the tourist board or the cultural institute; institutes of higher education might find that their attempts to attract talent from overseas are affected by the reputation of the products and services exported from the country or the behaviour of prominent athletes or media stars from the same country, and so on. National image is communicated through a complex web of channels and sectors, and none of the 'owners' of those channels have absolute control over all the factors that affect their interests.

In synthesis, I think it is helpful to consider Public Diplomacy as having three distinct stages of evolution or sophistication. Stage I Public Diplomacy is 'pre-Murrow' PD, where PD officers are simply charged to 'sell' whatever policies the administration chooses to implement. A comment from a U.S. government official to a PD officer which appeared in John Brown's *Public Diplomacy Press Review* perfectly characterizes Stage I PD:

> Look, you just forget about policy, that's not your business; we'll make the policy and then you can put it on your damn radios.[12]

Stage II Public Diplomacy is the 'post-Murrow' stage, where the function is basically still to 'sell' government policies, but PD officers are 'in at the take-offs', and thus have some power to condition the style and indeed the content of foreign policy.

There is a parallel here in the commercial sector when branding becomes fully represented in the boardroom: here, the marketing function is recognized as the corporation's 'eyes and ears on the ground' and its link with the marketplace, not merely informing strategy but actually driving innovation and new product development.

Stage III Public Diplomacy, which is the direction today favoured by the United Kingdom's Foreign and Commonwealth Office, uses the tools of PD in a different way altogether, and has seldom been consistently or well used by governments: this is Public Diplomacy as an *instrument of policy*, rather than as a method of communication. Here, a wide range of non-military methods (which include but are not necessarily limited to communications techniques) are used in order to bring about changes in the behaviours of populations, either in order to cause them to bring about policy changes through democratic influence over their own governments, or even by direct action.

The appeal of such an instrument of 'soft power' hardly needs emphasizing. For a country desiring regime change in another country, for example, the prospect of being able to persuade the other country's population to replace their own government is incomparably preferable (not to mention far cheaper) than doing it by direct military intervention. Not surprisingly, there have been numerous attempts in the past to achieve such ends, ranging from deliberate rumour-mongering to fake broadcasting; and some real successes have been achieved through the use of cultural diplomacy, although of course the effectiveness of such methods is notoriously hard to measure as cultural influence is always a slow-burning and indirect influence.

Few now dispute that the deliberate dissemination of American popular culture into the Soviet Union played a part in helping to defeat Communism, and many would argue that when the struggle is genuinely an ideological one – as was the case during the Cold War – then cultural diplomacy may well be a more appropriate weapon than warfare. Given that the biggest threats to world peace today are primarily ideological in nature, it seems surprising that the lessons of the Cold War appear not to have been well learned. Where culture is the problem, culture is also likely to be the solution.

In the modern age, it also seems natural that governments should turn to the world of commerce for guidance in this area, since creating wide-scale changes in opinion and behaviour through persuasion rather than coercion, through attraction rather than compulsion, is seen to be the essence of branding and marketing. To 'brand' democracy, for example, and thus create widespread 'purchase' of the democratic 'product' in undemocratic countries, would surely be the least harmful, most cost-effective and most benign instrument of foreign policy that human ingenuity could devise. It would indeed be a mark of human progress if nations could discover ways of *persuading* each other to change their behaviour – and only when this is necessary for the greater good, of course: the peak of human civilization would occur when such interventions evolved from violent, to peaceful, to non-existent.

But there are many obstacles to such a state of affairs. Conventional commercial branding depends to a large extent on open access to widely-consumed commercial media, a condition that by definition is usually lacking in undemocratic countries; and finding ways to achieve a substantial branding effect *without* the use of media is indeed an interesting challenge, which without the increasing reach of the internet might seem entirely beyond the realms of possibility.

Who you are, how you are seen, and what you do, are all questions which are intimately and perhaps inextricably linked, which is why no state can hope to achieve its aims in the modern world without a mature and sophisticated fusion of Public Diplomacy and competitive identity.

CHAPTER 8

'Brand Europe' – Where Next?

Various past editions of the Anholt Nation Brands Index have included a 'guest slot', so that in addition to the 35–50 countries which have been regularly monitored in the survey, it has been possible to take a global snapshot of perceptions of any other country which happened to be of interest at any particular time. Two of the guest slots have featured Israel and Iran, countries whose exceptionally poor scores in the NBI provoked a great deal of interest, commentary and controversy, and which have been briefly covered in earlier chapters of this book.

For the Second Quarter of 2006, I decided to devote the 'guest slot' not to a country, but to the European Union. Fourteen of the 25 members of the EU were already included in the NBI at this point, so we had a clear picture of how they ranked as individual 'brands', but no sense of worldwide attitudes to 'Brand Europe' as a whole. It therefore seemed like a good idea to use the NBI to measure Europe's overall reputational health.

From the point of view of the 26,500 respondents in 35 countries that I polled on their perceptions of Europe, a large and diverse region is a rather different proposition from a nation-state, and it is correspondingly harder to offer general opinions about it. Nonetheless, a fascinating picture emerged of how the world sees Europe.

Very favourably indeed, was the clear verdict. This was a surprising result to some people, especially within Europe itself, where the EU is not always thought of as an admired or even aspirational global 'brand'. In fact, the European Union took first place in the ranking in the NBI, above the United Kingdom, the previous top scorer. The region scored no top rankings on any of the individual points of the nation brand hexagon, but its performance was sufficiently strong and consistent to give it a higher overall score than any of the 35 countries in the list.

In one sense, this should come as no surprise. If Europe is perceived as the sum total of its member states, one would certainly expect it to be highly ranked: more than half of the top 20 nations in the survey are always European. Few places in the world could be more attractive than a composite of Italy plus France plus the UK plus Germany plus Sweden, and so forth.

And here is the point. One of Europe's many reputational issues is a technical one: the word 'Europe' can mean quite different things to different people in different contexts, and it's sometimes quite hard to know which 'brand' one is actually measuring. For many people in Asia and the Pacific, the Americas, the Middle East and Africa, 'Europe' simply refers to the continent of Europe – in other words, a fairly loose geographical, historical and cultural entity rather than a precise political one. For these populations, the idea of 'Europe' embraces a wide range of attractive concepts, including a wonderful collection of desirable consumer brands (think German cars and domestic appliances, plus Italian and French food, fashion and lifestyle, plus Swiss technology, plus Scandinavian design), one of the most attractive clusters of desirable tourism and cultural destinations, a bloc of some of the world's most stable democratic governments, several of the biggest economies in the world, and so forth.

The fact that we specified 'The European Union' rather than just 'Europe' in the survey didn't appear to affect this perception – informal research suggests that many people in other parts of the world simply take 'The European Union' to be an official name for the continent of Europe. People are also relatively imprecise about which countries are perceived to be European (because they are on the continent of Europe) and which are actually members of the European Union.

This perception of Europe-as-continent only changes when we specifically asked questions about governance: here, respondents were compelled to think about the governance of the European Union as a region rather than as a group of separate states, and on this point of the hexagon the average ranking of the EU is ninth, by far its lowest score. A picture begins to emerge of very high esteem for Europe-as-continent and relatively low esteem for Europe-as-institution.

For Europeans, 'The European Union' isn't the same thing at all as the continent of Europe, and their strongest associations are with Europe-as-institution. For them, the phrase 'European Union' stands unequivocally for the political and administrative machinery of Europe, and is associated by some Europeans with factors that are at best tedious and worst dysfunctional, even corrupt: bureaucracy gone mad, reams of petty and interfering legislation, outdated ideologies, and so on. These are doubtless the same associations that prompted a majority of Dutch and French voters to reject the Constitutional Treaty in 2005.

Not surprisingly, there is a distinction in viewpoint between the long-standing member states and the more recent and future accession states. For the latter, the brand image of Europe is associated with prosperity, with finally joining the 'community of free nations', an act of closure for the ex-Soviet states.

How the world sees Europe

Table 8.1 shows how each of the 35 countries in the Nation Brands Index ranks the EU for each point of the Nation Brands Hexagon. The data shows that the broad perception is of the EU as a region of opportunity: most people in most countries see it as a good place to live, work and study. Its industry and research and development are seen as strong; people value having Europeans both as friends and as senior employees. Again, EU governance is not seen so positively, particularly by its own citizens, but this is not a serious problem area. The rankings for European contemporary culture are strong, but perhaps unexpectedly, heritage and tourism – including the welcome our respondents expect to receive from European people – are its weakest areas.

The countries where people rate the brand image of Europe most highly (1st, 2nd or 3rd place) include four of the founding members of the Union (Belgium, France, Germany and Italy), some

Table 8.1 How the world sees Europe

RANKING OF EU'S BRAND DIMENSIONS BY THE 35 PANEL COUNTRIES
IN THE ANHOLT NATION BRANDS INDEX (QUARTER 2, 2006)

	ALL QUESTIONS	Exports	Governance	Culture/ heritage	People	Tourism	Investment/ immigration
ALL COUNTRIES	**1**	**4**	**9**	**7**	**4**	**7**	**4**
Argentina	1	4	10	6	6	4	3
Czech Rep.	1	3	9	4	2	4	1
Egypt	1	4	4	4	6	4	1
Poland	1	3	9	4	1	6	1
Portugal	1	4	10	10	2	3	1
Russia	1	3	9	4	2	6	3
Brazil	2	3	6	5	7	7	2
Hungary	2	4	13	3	1	2	2
Belgium	2	1	9	3	5	4	3
France	2	4	9	2	6	7	3
Germany	2	3	7	2	7	5	2
Ireland	2	3	4	10	6	6	2
Italy	2	3	9	2	3	2	2
Spain	2	4	7	3	2	3	2
Switzerland	2	3	10	5	6	10	3
China	3	3	5	6	4	5	3
Indonesia	3	4	3	6	3	10	3
Mexico	3	4	15	7	5	6	3
India	4	6	8	4	8	3	6
Netherlands	4	4	12	11	9	17	3
Turkey	4	3	6	4	11	8	2

Table 8.1 How the world sees Europe – *continued*

RANKING OF EU'S BRAND DIMENSIONS BY THE 35 PANEL COUNTRIES
IN THE ANHOLT NATION BRANDS INDEX (QUARTER 2, 2006)

	ALL QUESTIONS	Exports	Governance	Culture/heritage	People	Tourism	Investment/immigration
Singapore	5	7	9	10	10	5	7
South Africa	5	5	12	9	10	8	6
South Korea	5	5	3	7	8	8	8
Estonia	7	4	11	12	6	7	2
Norway	7	8	11	13	12	8	7
UK	7	5	12	11	10	16	6
Japan	9	6	7	7	12	14	9
New Zealand	9	7	9	11	12	4	8
Sweden	9	5	12	15	15	20	7
Canada	10	6	10	11	14	13	10
Malaysia	10	5	11	14	11	13	8
Australia	11	9	12	10	13	16	8
USA	12	8	13	12	17	18	11
Denmark	16	7	11	20	15	21	7

Source: www.nationbrandsindex.com

later accessions (Ireland, Portugal, the Czech Republic, Poland, Spain and Hungary), a small group of far-flung countries (Argentina, Brazil, China, Indonesia and Mexico), Egypt, Russia and Switzerland. Turkey, one of the EU's aspirant member states, is just outside this positive group, ranking Europe in 4th place. The Netherlands, the only other 1952 member of the original ECSC (apart from Luxembourg where the NBI is not carried out), also ranks the EU in overall 4th place, with noticeably lower scores on several points of the hexagon than its founding partners.

The countries with the least positive perceptions of Europe (those which rank the EU in 7th place or lower) include Sweden, Denmark and the persistently Euro-sceptic Norway – although it is interesting to note that our non-EU Norwegian panel is more favourably inclined towards the EU than the EU member states Sweden and Denmark. Nordic-leaning Estonia also ranks the EU poorly; the UK (bearing out the result noted in previous editions that the UK panel consistently ranks other English-speaking Commonwealth countries higher than its European partners); the old Commonwealth countries themselves (Australia, New Zealand and Canada), the United States (where respondents really only rank the EU highly as a provider of branded products), Malaysia and Japan.

Taking the governance dimension, the picture changes somewhat. There are fewer EU countries in the most positive group: only Ireland and Spain (both of which are acknowledged to have done well economically out of their membership) and Germany rank the EU higher than 9th for governance, whereas 7 non-European countries plus Turkey are in this group. Those least positive about EU governance include Hungary and Netherlands. The investment/ immigration picture is closer to the all-question one. One exception is that Estonia moves up to join the other new accession states in the most positive group.

Some other results are interesting at a more detailed level: for example Holland's and Denmark's strong lack of identification with the EU in terms of its culture, its people and tourism. Portugal, Ireland and the UK – three Atlantic nations – similarly do not seem to warm to the rest of the EU culturally, unlike the Treaty of Rome heartlands and Spain.

Defining 'brand Europe'

There was a great deal of debate about the image of Europe, both internally and externally, in the year of its 50th anniversary. Even the European Commission, in the week before the Q2 edition of the 2005 NBI went to press, announced a Europe-wide student competition to design a new logo and slogan for Europe in celebration of the 50th anniversary of the Treaty of Rome. The decision to base the competition on a 'brand identity' was no coincidence: for young people especially, Europe is undergoing something of an identity crisis, and it would certainly be most convenient if Europe suddenly found itself able to unite under a single slogan and a single logo. (The chances of such a consensus occurring are undoubtedly greater if the proposal originates with innocent young people rather than the Commission itself, or one of the member states).

The competition was just a piece of fun, but it does reflect an important point about the reputation of places: just like commercial and corporate brands, a powerful brand identity tends to stem from a powerful and united sense of common purpose within the organization itself. Ask any company about its brand, and it may well talk first about its corporate culture – how the staff 'live the brand' – rather than questions of external promotion and publicity.

So just in case anybody should fall into the trap of thinking that logos and slogans can achieve anything more significant than mild publicity for an important anniversary, the point needs to be stressed that without a common purpose there can be no community, and without community there can be no identity. One reason why the brand image of Europe-as-institution falls so far short of the powerful 'natural' brand of Europe-as-continent is because the region is lacking a powerful and widely-agreed *internal* brand, a sense of common purpose and common identity. Asking for logos and slogans for Europe at this stage is like walking into a restaurant and asking for the bill – it is most certainly doing things the wrong way round.

When the memory of two world wars was still fresh in people's minds, Europe did not have this problem because its founding principles of ensuring lasting peace and prosperity were highly relevant.

Today, the EU is suffering the price of its own success: it has gone so far towards creating peace and prosperity that it may have done itself out of a job, or at least done itself out of a defining purpose.

And yet Europe's new defining purposes are plainly there, and merely need to be stated, to be crystallized, and for people to rally around them in some semblance of consensus. Europe finds itself once again at the heart of at least two issues which threaten global stability, and even global survival, just as surely as it did in the first half of the twentieth century. The challenge of meeting climate change is one in which Europe could claim to have both a particular responsibility, and a particular competence; and the increasing tensions between the Muslim world and 'the West', and the critical need to avoid the self-fulfilling prophecy of labelling this as a clash of civilizations, is nowhere more visible than in Turkey's EU accession process, and in the ways in which most EU member states are now struggling with updating their own national identities to include expanding immigrant populations from different regions, different cultures and different religions.

The challenge for all countries in Europe and beyond is to find ways of continually presenting and re-presenting their past cultural achievements alongside their modern equivalents in ways that are fresh, relevant and appealing to younger audiences. This task is made ever more complex by the increasing plurality of modern societies – to celebrate the glories of a typically somewhat mono-cultural past without marginalizing or seeming to ignore the multi-racial reality of the country's modern day population is a real quandary for most countries. Still, since the only solution is to give equal emphasis to present-day cultural enterprise, it is basically a productive dilemma, because it lessens the temptation for countries to rest on their laurels and live in the past.

Race is a critical factor in national and regional identity, and indeed is one of the main reasons why so many countries – richer European countries in particular – need to start thinking very hard about how well their traditional international image reflects their present reality, even though that image might appear to be in very good shape. Perhaps this is one part of the explanation for France's current racial tensions: the 'brand story' of France, the way the country is viewed, and to some extent the way it still represents itself to the outside world, is still an old story of a white Christian European power. But many French people who are neither white nor Christian feel that the national story leaves them out: and of course that causes bitter internal resentment as well as impacting on the country's external reputation. France's scores for governance in the Nation Brands Index, indeed, have on several occasions dropped quite noticeably following international media focus on its inner-city disturbances; and the NBI is a survey which is notable for the almost unwavering stability of its results.

Many countries now need to reassess the way they identify themselves and communicate that identity to the world in the light of their changing populations. It's one of the biggest tasks facing governments today, and is an acute challenge for the way in which countries and regions understand and manage their external reputation and internal purpose.

Another reason for the EU's weak 'brand image' is the long-standing habit of member state governments to ascribe all successes to their own country and all failures to the EU. It is certainly not impossible for people to feel multiple loyalties – to community, to region, to country, to continent – but wherever those loyalties are weakest, it provides an opportunity for politicians to use the place as a scapegoat or dumping-ground for anything unwanted, negative or undesirable, and over time this habit will further weaken and eventually kill the brand.

Finally, if a strong image is the result of a place proving itself to be competent, innovative and attractive on all points of the hexagon, the EU as an institution really only fires on one cylinder: it seldom touches its own populations through any of the points of the hexagon that really inspire them (culture, tourism, people, business and brands) but, as a body whose primary function is regulatory, through the one that they are most likely to find boring or unwelcome (governance).

The identity task for Europe is therefore mainly an internal one: to define what its job must be for the next 50 years, and to generate consensus, passion and ambition around this. Unless this purpose is relevant, credible and inspiring to people in the areas that they care about most, the brand of Europe-as-institution will never be more than a weak shadow of the brand of Europe-as-continent.

Perception, whether we like it or not, is inseparable and often indistinguishable from reality. Unless the institutions of Europe can learn to treat the issues of identity and reputation with as much gravity and respect as they do the 'harder' issues, they may find that real progress on Europe's most significant challenges will remain beyond their reach.

As I write in 2009, a global economic recession is well under way, and such concerns have to some extent receded into the background. Many now would say that questions about the image of the EU and Europe – or the images of member states – are simply trivial when compared with the harsh facts of economic survival, and that the whole business of understanding and managing public perceptions is a luxury that can only be afforded in times of growth and prosperity.

I would argue the opposite: we live in a world in which perceptions regularly trump reality – the current economic crisis is surely proof of that – and today it's all about the survival of those *perceived to be* the fittest. Knowing how to deal with intangibles is just as important in such times as traditional military or monetary competence.

Today, the consequences of intangibles are frighteningly tangible. The big challenges facing us today – climate change, global recession, violent extremism – are complex in nature, but clearly have one thing in common: none of them can be tackled in conventional ways. The so-called 'war on terror' self-evidently can't be won with conventional weapons because it's a battle of values and identity, played out in the media as much as in the battleground. Climate change can't easily be slowed down with legal or fiscal solutions because it's an international problem which is intimately linked to people's lifestyles and behaviours. Recession, or depression, is as much about consumer confidence as it is about toxic debts. The 'demographic time-bomb' is as much about how different generations view their role in society, and vice-versa, as it is about welfare provision and employment law.

The real battlegrounds are ideas, values, beliefs, behaviours, perceptions. We humans have souls as well as bodies, and our behaviour is often influenced more by the former than the latter. As Robert Gates, now America's new Secretary of Defence, stated in a 2007 lecture,

> These [asymmetric] conflicts will be fundamentally political in nature, and require the application of all elements of national power. Success will be less a matter of imposing one's will and more a function of shaping behaviour – of friends, adversaries, and most importantly, the people in between.[13]

This is the spirit of the age we live in, and a glance at the ideas emerging on any one day will confirm this: the New Economics Foundation in London publishes a paper on *National Accounts of Wellbeing;* a NATO official repeats that Afghanistan is a 'battle of hearts and minds'; yet another commentator refers to Bhutan's model of Gross National Happiness. We are probably not witnessing the 'death of capitalism' (the emerging global middle class is too vast, too powerful and too attached to its tantalizing taste of prosperity to be prepared to let it go), but we do seem to be moving towards a more human and humanistic account of our world, and – dare I say it – a post-neoliberal age.

To a great extent, the institutions of European member states already reflect the growing emphasis on identity and perception in international affairs. Most European Ministries of Foreign Affairs are now actively involved in Public Diplomacy, and some of them have been for a number of years. Today, it is well recognized that diplomats must be experts in media management, export and investment promotion and cultural relations as much as policy matters. Many European nations are rightly proud of their diplomatic services, and their transition to a more modern, more flexible, more media-aware public diplomacy, although slow and painful, is quite rapid.

The British Council, the Goethe Institute, the Swedish Institute, the Instituto Cervantes, the Czech Centres, the Instituto Camões, the Alliance Française and the other European cultural institutes have been working internationally for decades, in many cases unknown to their domestic taxpayers, improving their countries'

– and consequently Europe's – relationships and reputations with other populations through cultural exchange. This kind of influence, although slowly and laboriously built, is highly effective, for the simple reason that it's hard to hate somebody you know well: and you get to know other peoples best through their culture. It is often argued that such groundwork is the essential, indispensable and irreplaceable means of resolving, avoiding and mitigating hatred and ignorance between peoples: where culture is the problem, culture is also the solution.

The BBC, Radio France Internationale and Deutsche Welle are amongst the most trusted voices in international broadcasting, still relied on by millions of listeners and viewers in almost every country on earth for unbiased information as well as quality culture and entertainment. Europe's creative industries – including the persuasive arts of advertising, marketing, design and public relations – are recognized as the best in the world. Most of the world's aid and development assistance comes from Europe; most of the best-known non-governmental organizations – such as Oxfam, Christian Aid, Médicins sans Frontières, Save the Children, the Red Cross – are European; all of this is 'soft' power too, because helping people to achieve prosperity, education, good governance and health in poor and conflicted states does more to tackle violent extremism in the long term than military action does in the immediate term, and usually does it more cost-effectively too.

Such instruments are in reality far from soft: intellectual, communicative, creative, persuasive, spiritual and cultural power is tangible, measurable, and profound in its effects. It is telling that Joseph Nye, the Harvard academic who originally coined the phrase 'soft power', now prefers to use the phrase 'smart power'.

All this work is well inside Europe's comfort zone, the zone where much of our really precious experience lies. In smart power, Europe can reasonably claim to outgun the rest of the world, and to possess skills and resources that are critically necessary and in critically short supply. Relationships with America and other blocs of power built on this happy coincidence of supply and demand might be more equal and more productive than we could ever hope to achieve as a half-hearted and woefully uncoordinated partner in the delivery of military or economic brute force.

During a visit to Afghanistan in the Summer of 2008, I was shocked – although not altogether surprised – to note the profound differences in attitude, in aspirations, in techniques, in style and in expectations between the various European forces in the coalition: these clearly reflected profound cultural differences, and are a major component of the inefficiency and lack of coordination between the allies.

Critics of interventions such as the NATO operation in Afghanistan often speak of the 'opportunity cost' they represent, listing the numerous, and equally pressing trouble-spots around the world where the international community is unable to provide developmental or military assistance because of the cost of such conflicts. But I cannot help feeling that if our multilateral institutions were able to operate in a manner which was, for the sake of argument, 60% efficient rather than 60% inefficient, the international community would have relatively little difficulty in covering most of the really vital conflicts and pressure-points.

These problems are not principally hardware problems: they are 'soft' problems of cultural and ideological difference, messaging and communication, coordination and shared purpose. And indeed the fundamental problems of Afghanistan itself are, like so many of today's conflicts, ideological and cultural in nature; the long-term solutions are much more likely to be developmental, educational and political than military. Again, what is urgently needed is intellectual and cultural competence; Europe should be a paragon of such smart power, and yet it delivers sporadically at best.

Like most countries in history, the European nations have invested most and continue to spend most on hard power, even though it is demonstrably only part of the solution to most problems. In the past, European governments and their armies have developed many forms of 'kinetic' warfare to great levels of sophistication. Yet despite the overwhelming evidence that such warfare is entirely inadequate on its own, we have generally avoided giving the same attention to soft power. Boys prefer toys, while social science is complicated and (to some) tedious and bewildering too. And it seldom goes bang or makes people and buildings fall over.

Yet all the *components* of a sophisticated grasp of the persuasive skills lie within our reach: they still need to be assembled into a coherent and functioning system. We **have** psychology, anthropology, sociology, linguistics, neuroscience, ethics, behavioural research, rhetoric, propaganda, media studies, marketing communications, brand strategy, public affairs, public diplomacy, cultural relations and much else besides: what we don't have is a science of influence that binds them all together and makes them *work*. We need a system that converts these fundamentally analytical tools into operative mechanisms, and where better than Europe to forge this new post-industrial revolution?

Soft power does not, of course, replace hard power. We all have our obligations to our allies and to our citizens and we still need to defend ourselves, and carry out essential peacekeeping roles in and occasionally beyond our neighbourhood. Hard power is unquestionably another human necessity. My hope is simply to urge the development of soft power – understanding it and wielding it effectively, responsibly and efficiently – at least to the same level as hard power, so that Europe has both tools in its toolbox.

It's time for Europe to give these other skills their due importance, and to work hard at improving our performance in this area. Individually, the member states of Europe wield the most important soft power capability on the planet, but collectively, Europe is far less than the sum of its parts.

We urgently need to pool our resources to create a credible joint strike capability in smart power. Europe needs a regional cultural body, a ministry of soft power, and needs to invest heavily in the infrastructure and institutions that will combine and multiply the region's capability in cultural relations, public diplomacy, and other forms of persuasive power.

Far from diminishing Europe's influence, such an investment will greatly improve our ability to contribute to the challenges of our age. We need to arm ourselves for the struggles that lie ahead.

CHAPTER 9

Public Sector, Private Sector

Recent history is littered with abortive attempts to apply the tricks, techniques and initiatives of corporations to the public sector, and although the performance of such knowledge transfers in many sectors is gradually improving with accumulated experience, public/private partnerships seem more commonly associated with failure than with success.

Admiring glances have often been cast by those in government and civil services at the creativity, speed, efficiency and lack of ceremony with which companies appear able to hire and fire, restructure, reconstitute and reinvent themselves, build and implement strategies, raise and spend capital, create consensus, develop new products and get them to market, respond to competition, and react to disasters. Being answerable to shareholders seems vastly preferable to being accountable to taxpayers and voters; the higher salaries play a part in that admiration; and the ability to hold office for as long as you are competent to hold it seems like paradise.

What impresses politicians, as they struggle to squeeze a few extra votes from an increasingly apathetic electorate, is the apparent ability of certain companies to shape public discourse, to manipulate their own images at will, and above all to inspire unwavering respect, loyalty, even love for their brands. It is this power which more than any other feeds the vigorous public-private trade at the heart of the rapidly growing fields of place branding and public diplomacy.

This power, it must be said, is partly imaginary: the main reason why companies find it easier to be popular with their audiences is simply that they are offering something which that audience actually wants. With a willing interlocutor, a dialogue of sorts is relatively simple to achieve, and thus also a measure of control over one's own image.

The private sector, by contrast, is seldom heard to envy the public sector: the longing glances cast in this direction are most often from consultants and other service providers perceiving what they imagine to be the limitless fee-paying potential of public money, combined with the relative inexperience of government clients in defending themselves against smart consultants.

The will and the need for governments to learn from private-sector experience are undoubted, but the problems attendant on transferring skills from one sector to the other are particularly intractable because they are partly caused by certain basic cultural differences between corporations and government.

As I described in *Competitive Identity,* the main difference between companies and countries is that companies aren't really demo-cracies at all: in fact, they are a species of tolerated tyranny, in which the Chief Executive will seldom admit any deviation from the declared corporate or brand 'vision'. A social contract is a very different thing from a contract of employment, and a worker who disagrees or fails to respect corporate aims can either leave, or be fired. It is no accident that many of the places which have made the fastest and most noticeable progress in 'branding' themselves are the ones that are run most like corporations – most prominently city-states like Dubai and Singapore, where a Chief Executive-style leader has more than average ability to lay down the law and ensure adherence to his particular vision of the place and its future. Under such conditions, both the 'product' itself and the way in which it is 'made' and 'delivered' are subject to sufficient control or influence for a recognizable version of commercial brand management to take place.

In general, companies these days are encouraged to have ideo-logies, a notion that for very good reasons is rather frowned upon in the community of nations. (Cities, it should be said, are a rather different case, and perhaps because they are intrinsically less 'polit-ical' than countries, can often get away with a rather corporate-style management, complete with single vision and even uniform visual identity). The Chief Executives of companies are prized for their charisma, imagination, strength of character and – even in 2009 – a touch of ruthlessness, while the electorates of most democratic countries today show a decided preference for competent technocrats, whose qualities are judged by their ability to 'deliver' rather than to dream.

In many ways, such choices are the sign of a healthy and stable democracy and certainly shouldn't be sneered at, but the unavoidable consequence is that work within the governments and civil services of such countries becomes somewhat routine and repetitive. Indeed, in many richer countries, it can seem as if the main function of the civil service is to prevent change. Thus, the incentive for public sector workers and even government ministers to be truly creative, imaginative or entrepreneurial is rather low.

One should not be misled by the fact that the same style of management vocabulary is often heard in both sectors – the language, at least, of private enterprise has succeeded in permeating government as it has so many other sectors of society – but in government the buzz-words may mean something rather different. When a Chief Executive encourages his or her staff to 'think out of the box', it usually is a sincere invitation to radical thinking, from a complete revision of the company's product line or target market to outsourcing production to another country; when civil servants are given the same injunction by their departmental head, a 'dress-down Friday' may be more the kind of suggestion that is expected.

David Steven uses the metaphor of 'venture capitalists versus bankers' to describe how governments need to reform their culture in order to function and prosper in the age of global media.[14] A banker will tend to invest relatively small amounts of money in a large number of projects, all of which are expected to provide modest returns. Staff are not encouraged to take risks, and a project that fails will likely result in the sacking of the employee responsible for taking it on. Venture capitalists, on the other hand, tend to make large investments in small numbers of high-risk projects; imagination and even failure are respected; and the one or two projects that don't fail will provide more than adequate returns to bankroll the failures.

This risk culture is very much the keynote of modern public diplomacy, as the competition for consumer attention has never been more acute. As diplomacy's key 'audience' spreads out from the balanced, well-informed and fact-oriented professional élite of past ages to a wider, more emotive, impatient and often cynical mass audience, such a culture change becomes essential. The usual modest recipe of most government 'communications' projects – a conference here, a seminar there, some carefully-worded press releases sent out to carefully-selected journalists – may cost relatively little, but today run the risk of wasting every penny that is spent on them because such timid attempts to capture the imagination of a fickle and information-saturated public will seldom achieve anything at all.

Public diplomacy needs to be as fast-moving, as demotic and as compelling as the most popular of popular culture, and a campaigning mentality becomes the order of the day. Even diplomats, according to Daryl Copeland,[15] must become a species of guerrilla in order to operate effectively in this new landscape. One is no long queuing politely with other government officials for the measured attention of a minister or ambassador, so much as fighting for seconds of the public's attention against 'Big Brother', iTunes and Second Life. Public Diplomacy isn't just a slightly modified form of traditional diplomacy: it's a different ball game entirely, where entirely different rules apply.

Countries and companies are also in direct competition with each other for the attention of the same audiences, and it is precisely because of the skill of companies in gaining this attention that the contest has become so fierce.

From the point of view of companies trying to sell their products and services in the global marketplace, gaining that attention is certainly harder work than it used to be. In consequence, the emphasis placed on creativity – always the hardest and most important part of creating commercial communications – has steadily increased over the last few decades. This is partly because advertising and other forms of commercial communication are now a far more pervasive phenomenon in most people's lives than they used to be, and people have gradually built up resistance to it.

Once, consumers were prepared to put some effort into reading and understanding commercial messages, and even into political messages, because it is a natural tendency to listen to what people are saying to you: but once the messages began to proliferate beyond their ability to attend to everything that was directed at them, and they learned that there was seldom much value to be derived from these messages, consumers acquired the trick of shutting their minds to them. Consequently, advertisers need to use more and more sophisticated tricks in order to persuade people that, contrary to all expectations, this time the message really *is* worth listening to.

In the 1950s and 1960s, creativity in advertising was just the icing on the cake. An advertisement which showed the product, gave the information, looked good and was well placed, was sufficient for its purpose: but if it also managed to communicate the message in a winsome, witty and original way, then the advertiser could reap a substantial bonus in extra attention, interest, goodwill and sales. Now, most companies acknowledge that cutting-edge creativity is the cost of entry into most markets. Unless every piece of communication is truly striking, original, beautifully produced and utterly persuasive, it fails because no-one will even notice it: it simply won't register on the consumer's radar and will vanish without trace, along with the considerable investment the advertiser has made in developing and exposing it.

Consumers are bombarded every moment of every day with astonishing graphics, astounding utterances, the diligent application of remarkable amounts of intelligence, money, skill and hard work onto every tiny marketing problem, and this is what governments, tourist boards, cultural bodies and other communicators in the public sector have to compete against today – with, of course, the additional handicap that what they are trying to 'sell' is often of little interest to the consumer.

In effect, there is an unspoken pact between consumers and advertisers: consumers are only prepared to give a moment of their increasingly precious attention to messages if in return they are rewarded by being genuinely informed, having their emotions genuinely stirred, or by being genuinely entertained. This is the price of their voluntarily parting with some of their hard-won spare time in order to hear someone try to persuade them to part with their hard-earned cash – or, as it may be, their vote, their respect, their approval. And over the last half-century, as the consumer's attention has become a more and more valuable commodity, its price worldwide has steadily risen.

Public bodies are not battling it out alone with companies for this scarce resource. During the same period, another even more redoubtable opponent has emerged: the non-governmental organization. Many NGOs have been signally more effective at adopting and refining the communications techniques of corporations for their own purposes than governments have, and indeed at developing many entirely original approaches to the problem of message fatigue. Growing up in the intensely competitive 'attention marketplace' of the last 30 years, charities, pressure groups, campaigning groups, independent think-tanks and a whole host of other bodies and organizations – including, one could well argue, terrorist groups and fundamentalist movements – have quickly evolved into lean, efficient, media-literate and utterly communications-driven specialists. Like official bodies, these organizations have also faced the fundamental challenge that the 'product' they are 'selling' is intrinsically less appealing than that of their competitors in the commercial sector – indeed, in many cases, it is positively unwelcome – and many of them have risen to this challenge in spectacularly successful measure. Even more remarkably, most of them have achieved this despite the additional handicap of very limited budgets and human resources, which is how they have developed the additional and equally redoubtable skill of highly effective fund-raising and volunteer recruitment.

A large part of the reason why such organizations have risen so quickly and so effectively to the challenge of competing in the modern attention market is that their structures and cultures are inherently suited to the age in which they operate. Governments, civil services, and to a lesser extent corporations too, have the far greater challenge of having to adapt and change large fixed structures to the new reality, without losing the resource or the capability to continue dealing with the traditional issues and challenges which still form such a large part of their responsibility.

The best NGOs are successful because they are hybrid organizations, combining the intellectual rigour, research-based knowledge, political expertise, and broad strategic overview of governments, with the speed, efficiency, aggression, media and communications literacy, the same instinct for public opinion and the same passionate commitment to an ideological or quasi-ideological cause, as companies in the commercial marketplace. They also have the significant advantage of focus, the ability to specialize exclusively and intensively on a single issue or set of issues, while government departments are always compelled to be generalists to some degree. The only remedy that governments have to combat this terrifying level of expertise is to hire ever more consultants and special advisors, but too much 'bolted-on' expertise tends to slow things down and reduce rather than enhance the ability for them to make quick and reliable decisions.

It seems evident, then, that for governments to compete on equal terms with such bodies, they too will have to build their own hybrid cultures. Radically changing their own structures and cultures will take too long, and runs the risk of reducing their ability to deal with their more traditional – and still essential – roles and responsibilities.

This is one of the reasons why, together with my colleagues at the UK's Public Diplomacy Board, I devised 'PDLab', a public diplomacy resource which is deliberately situated and staffed outside the Foreign and Commonwealth Office. PDLab is predicated on the observation that there is a need for radical thinking and major innovation in the way Public Diplomacy is performed in the UK and elsewhere: if PD is to win the respect it requires as a key component in the art of progressive, collaborative and peaceful international relations, then it is clearly necessary to push the thinking vigorously forwards. Yet most foreign services continue to work with a limited range of fairly conventional PD tools and techniques, some of which are little more than simple media relations, clumsily adapted from the private sector, and poorly suited to the modern world.

To develop new approaches and new tools will require a good deal of highly informed creative thinking, and it will be necessary to bring together a set of skills and perspectives which have never been harnessed before in this context. PDLab is designed as a public diplomacy 'skunkworks',[16] and aims to tap into a wide range of contributors including professional creatives from various marketing communications disciplines; journalists; interactive specialists; writers; propaganda scholars; psychologists, anthropologists and sociologists; political scientists and many others besides.

The experiment has only just begun, but I believe it is a step in the right direction. Society and government today face certain challenges which simply cannot be tackled with the conventional instruments of political, military or economic power alone: the domain in which the most significant developments of our age will unfailingly take place, for better or for worse, is the domain of global public opinion and public engagement. If the only effective agents in this space, and consequently the only real focus of public trust, are commercial organizations, limited-issue political pressure groups and extremists, it is difficult to imagine that civilization can go anywhere but backwards.

For this reason, the drive towards a more effective, more enlightened public diplomacy is very much more important than it may at first appear: it represents our best chance of ensuring that society in the future is guided by truly democratic principles and not by commercial self-interest, the political or cultural fads of the moment, or worst of all, by mob rule.

CHAPTER 10

The Media and National Image

There are two sorts of company in the world: those whose primary focus is always on developing a better product that people will want to buy because it's better, and those whose primary focus is always on finding more effective ways of making people buy the product they're selling.

There are usually examples of both in any industry, but the young industry of 'place branding' seems to have acquired or inherited an inordinate number of the latter in a very short time. Many of these, rather than offer guidance on how to improve the image or reputation of places, appear at first sight to offer something even more practical and concrete: an opportunity to promote the country directly in print media or television.

Government officials in various countries often tell me how they have been approached by 'researchers' who are 'looking into the possibility of producing a special feature' about their country and its unique holiday and/or investment climate, usually for a highly prestigious international newspaper or business magazine. It usually later transpires that the researchers in question are actually sales agents for a public relations, 'communications' or media sales firm which has a licence from the prestigious newspaper to produce paid-for advertising supplements in its name.

With the masthead brand of a centuries-old newspaper on their business cards, these salesmen travel the world, tricking inexperienced government officials in developing and least-developed countries into funding, subsidizing or supporting such supplements, claiming that this exercise in 'nation branding' will raise their country – notwithstanding poverty, crime, civil war, disease, political instability or corruption – to a new level of international respect and esteem, boosting aid, foreign investment and tourism.

Of course, no evidence is ever produced that such results will really occur, nor can it be produced, and in reality these kinds of advertising supplements, once produced, usually go straight into the bin when the reader opens the newspaper. But even if they do happen to be closely read by some readers, a single appearance in an obviously sponsored supplement can do very little to raise the profile or change the image of a country which that reader might never have heard of before, or which is strongly associated in his or her mind with decades of poverty, instability, corruption or violence.

In fact, the reading patterns of such supplements are probably like those of car brochures: the vast majority of people who read these brochures turn out to be the people who already own such a car and are simply looking for reassurance that they have made the right choice. Similarly, the majority of people who take the trouble to read an advertising supplement about a rather obscure country are probably the people who already have some reason to be interested in that country: either because they come from there, have family there, have recently visited it, or are already planning to do so.

But most government officials, especially in poorer countries, are inexperienced in the ways of the media. Their training is usually in political science or economics: most will have little direct experience of the private sector, and will know nothing of the arcana of advertising, public relations, media sales and brand management.

Of course, the media salespeople won't miss any opportunity to bandy around the thrilling and mysterious vocabulary of 'nation branding' and 'destination branding', citing the tremendous rise in interest in this important field, showing examples of stunning television and print campaigns produced by (very rich) developing countries as evidence of this new trend, and stoking up a strong sense of anxiety that no developing country can afford not to enter this new arms race of advertising and promotion.

Some of them, I discover, even quote my work in their sales pitches, carefully avoiding the passages where I inveigh against the wicked waste of taxpayers' and donors' funds in useless propaganda, citing instead the phrases where I stress the importance of a positive national reputation for economic, political and social development in a globally-connected world.

As revenues from display and recruitment advertising decline, and endless, instantly-updated news and comment are now freely available on the internet, traditional printed newspapers and magazines, as well as the traditional broadcast media, are desperately seeking other sources of revenue as they struggle to stave off their inevitable demise.[17] It's not surprising under such circumstances that the traditional 'Chinese Wall' between editorial and advertising has crumbled: not long ago, it was the pride of serious newspapers and television channels that not even their biggest advertisers could be sure of regular or uncritical editorial coverage in the same titles where they advertised. Today, the field is wide open for virtually any disguised or even quite blatant form of advertorial, product placement or other forms of endorsement, as long as the price is right and the newspaper or broadcaster stays within the law (and the law on such matters is, in most countries, a weak form of voluntary self-regulation at best).

In one recent case, officials from a government which I advise were approached by an advertising supplement salesman, claiming to be a journalist from a leading newspaper which was looking into the possibility of covering their country in yet another high-profile special report. Dangling this possibility, he instructed them to provide him with comprehensive details about the country's economy, including its principal companies and their directors' contact details. He even gave them a deadline for providing this information, stressing that the 'opportunity' of featuring their country would only be available for a limited time.

This request was, of course, impertinent nonsense: he could have found the economic information himself in five minutes on Wikipedia, and making them provide contact details for company directors simply saved him the trouble of producing his own hit-list of corporations to which he could sell advertising 'opportunities' within the supplement. By getting their details in this way, he could even claim to the companies that their names had been suggested to him by their government, giving the exercise a quasi-official endorsement and an aura of respectability.

All the classic tricks of the snake-oil salesman were there: suggesting that the salesman is doing the customer a favour by giving him the exclusive opportunity of acquiring the product; pretending that the product may not actually be on sale at all, and that there's only a small chance it might become available; failing to make any mention of cost until the moment of payment; making the purchaser work hard to 'deserve' the product; claiming that the offer is time limited.

The salesman even operated a classic pincer movement on the officials, by writing at the same time to the country's Prime Minister (in considerably more obsequious tones), praising him in rather vague terms for his enlightened vision for the country, quoting one of his recent speeches, and stating that the supplement was scheduled to coincide with an important international summit due to take place a few months later. In contrast to the correspondence with the officials, there was no suggestion in this letter that the country had to prove itself worthy of such a supplement – the decision to publish was presented as a *fait accompli*.

As it turned out, the salesman was wasting his time, as very few of the companies he approached in the country felt able or willing to 'invest' in advertising in the supplement, for the simple reason that almost none of them were exporters, and paying a lot of money to promote their goods to foreign audiences was patently absurd. After a frantic last attempt to persuade the government that they were now responsible for subsidizing the full cost of the supplement, he departed for his next developing country.

Similar tales often reach me of media sales people representing international TV channels who trick the governments of poor countries into spending tens of thousands or even hundreds of thousands of dollars on tiny numbers of TV commercials, dazzling them with the astronomical numbers of viewers these spots will reach around the world. And because such governments seldom have the experience to commission or the facilities to produce their own commercials, the TV channel will often earn extra fees by cobbling together the film themselves – taking advantage of the fact that few government officials understand the difference between the media sales arm of a TV channel and the creative department of a proper advertising agency.

More importantly, few of them understand the importance of scheduling – a TV spot that appears in off-peak time in the wealthy markets of Europe or North America won't hit many viewers – or the importance of frequency: one or two TV spots over the course of a few weeks are highly unlikely to register in any way at all on the viewer, something that only frequent repeats over many months, costing millions of dollars, can achieve.

It isn't just the innocence or inexperience of government officials that makes life easy for these itinerant salespeople: the reality is that it's enormously difficult for any government during its normal term of office to produce any measurable impact on their nation's international reputation – such things can take generations to shift – and the temptation to spend a lot of money on something as appealing, as tangible, as modern and as uplifting as an international advertising campaign is a strong temptation indeed. Producing and measuring real outcomes is terribly hard, especially in the short term; but producing and measuring outputs is child's play.

Of course the bigger question behind all this remains one of effectiveness: it's not simply a matter of whether these advertising 'opportunities' are being honestly and transparently sold or not, but also whether they actually do what they claim to do. As I have often stated in this book and elsewhere, I have yet to see any proof that mere messaging has any influence whatsoever on people's pre-existing ideas and prejudices about other countries. I can think of many reasons why they wouldn't, and nobody has yet produced any solid evidence to show me that they might.

None of this is helped by the fact that the multilateral institutions, development agencies, rich country governments and NGOs, in their efforts to appear up-to-date and innovative in their approaches to capacity building, poverty reduction and economic competitiveness, will, more and more often, enthusiastically endorse these media-based interpretations of 'nation branding' in developing countries. Just like the governments they advise, they may have little knowledge or understanding of the world of media, still less the difficult and unfamiliar subject of national image management (perhaps it would be more accurate to say the 'non-existent subject of national image management'), and regularly fall into the same traps as their clients, believing quite innocently and uncritically that the techniques that build big commercial brands in the rich world must surely be easily adaptable to building big country brands in the poor world.

It's another terrible example of the temptation and the corruption of aid: what could be more appropriate, more fun, more pleasing to the Western donors, or more appropriate to the culture of those donors, than to spend huge piles of Western money on Western-style 'communications'. The literature and the consultants' reports produced by the NGOs, the development agencies, the Western governments and the multilateral institutions are packed with references to 'communications' and the modern importance of 'soft power'. If an African government spends millions of dollars on television spots uselessly extolling carefully selected segments of its sparkling beaches, happy villages, gleaming hotels, factories, airports and skyscrapers (carefully editing out the slums in the background), isn't it simply doing what it's told?

It's truly the blind leading the blind, innocently or ignorantly conspiring together to waste billions of dollars of aid in futile state propaganda – and the only beneficiaries are the media, the PR and marketing agencies, and the various individuals along the route who pocket the commissions on each mega-deal.

What is abundantly clear is that governments, especially in the developing world, need to understand these matters better, and need to take more control over their relationships with the international media: how they use it, and how it uses them. For this reason, I often recommend that countries set up a national Media Centre with the remit of providing a professional interface between government, business, civil society and the international media. An outline of such a unit is described in the next section of this chapter.

The media needn't be and shouldn't be the enemy of governments that are interested in enhancing their international reputation – it is, after all, one of the main conduits through which national image usually travels. In some cases, even advertising supplements might be an appropriate component in the media mix used for promoting tourism or foreign investment – but only if they are part of a clear strategy, based on a clear definition of the target market, associated with clear criteria for measuring and evaluating success, based on a properly worked out budget, with proper mechanisms for ensuring that such activities are planned and executed creatively, cost-effectively and professionally.

Armed with such knowledge and preparation, governments wouldn't simply react to the first salesman who calls, but would analyze the various offerings, make their own selection on the basis of clear criteria, take the initiative and approach the best media themselves, and negotiate a proper deal in the interest of their taxpayers.

In the meantime, we can expect to see ethical and professional standards continue to plummet in the world's media, which is why it is all the more important that governments arm themselves with the expertise, experience and confidence to deal decisively and effectively with them.

Recently, I was shocked to see a prominent item during the main prime-time news programme of one very distinguished international TV channel, announcing the launch of a new product from an American company. The product was described in detail, listing all its features and benefits, the camera pausing respectfully for fully five seconds – an eternity in the fast-moving world of 24-hour TV news – over the manufacturer's logo. There was a lengthy interview with a senior executive from the company, extolling the virtues of the product. None of the manufacturer's competitors or their products were mentioned. There wasn't even an attempt to link the 'news' item to any broader topic of interest. It was, in short, an advertisement. I saw it repeated 12 times during the following 36 hours.

This is the future of the media: a space for black propaganda where paid-for promotion, objective information and comment become indistinguishable, where the real sponsors of the message are entirely disguised, and where, in consequence, no message can be taken on trust.

If this is the new editorial environment, it is surely only a matter of time – and the price being right – for paid political messages to find their space alongside the commercial ones. It is surely time to redouble our efforts not just to arm governments against media sales, but also to inoculate our children against believing anything they see on the television, the internet, or read in a newspaper over the course of their lifetimes.

The national Media Centre

Although the emphasis in enhancing the images and reputations of places should be on creating substance rather than communications, it has to be acknowledged that many countries, especially developing economies, are too passive and reactive in their dealings with the international media. Their responses to the media are often highly disconnected between the private and public sectors, and between sectors. The extreme vulnerability of public servants to the blandishments of media sales, as described in the previous section, is equally significant.

The creation of a national, centralized Media Centre is something I often recommend in these cases. This provides a single point of contact for all foreign media interested in covering the country in any context, and is a great help in harmonizing the messages going out to the media from the country.

In cases of negative coverage, the Media Centre should have a sophisticated, multilingual Crisis Management section which could issue accurate and timely rebuttals, consistent and responsible statements from all key players, and ensure that the media deals with the country as consistently and respectfully as possible.

The Media Centre should also be responsible for monitoring the international media for all significant mentions of the country, so that it can identify problems with as much advance warning as possible, and help all the relevant players to develop a consistent and effective strategy for dealing with the issue.

The Media Centre should be equipped with media monitoring and other forms of polling and research expertise and resources, and should take responsibility for survey instruments that are related to tracking and measuring the country's international image.

Those all-important visits to the country by journalists covering tourism, foreign investment, culture, exports, politics and other sectors can be planned and coordinated by the Media Centre, ensuring that proper information, hospitality, access and resources are provided. A club house (modelled on the Foreign Press Centres that are to be found in rich-country capitals around the world) where foreign journalists can visit, work, find information, help and hospitality, connectivity and contacts, is also a very valuable asset.

The Media Centre can also help to coordinate the messaging of the country's major communicators (tourist board, investment promotion agency, main exporters, Ministry of Foreign Affairs etc), and – if acceptable to all parties, even exercise some quality control over their productions, to make sure that no major sector carries out promotional or informational campaigns that are below acceptable international standards.

Bad press

It is a refrain I hear very often as I listen to governments complaining about how badly the international media treats them: that bad news seems to travel faster than good, and that getting a positive story into the media is virtually impossible.

Certainly, public opinion habitually assumes that negative stories in the media are more likely to be truthful than positive ones. Both journalists and readers often believe that if a story is to the disadvantage of the protagonist, then it is more likely that the 'real truth' has been discovered, and we have somehow been privileged to peep through a tear in the curtain of the official version. Any story that clearly benefits the reputation of an individual – or especially a government – must surely be mistrusted, because you don't get something for nothing in this world.

There is a growing habit of cynicism amongst the media in many countries which I'm afraid they caught from the British press: the notion that anyone in any position of power, influence or prosperity, anyone who succeeds at anything, anyone who is at all admired, anyone in a prominent or public position – indeed, anyone at all who is not clearly a victim or an underdog – must necessarily be lying about something, and the duty of the reporter is to identify and expose their lie, and not give up until they've found it (and if they really can't find it, then they will sometimes invent one, or hint that there's one which nobody has yet discovered). This crusading cynicism sits unhappily alongside the rapidly slipping integrity of their editorial 'product' as described in the previous section.

In some cases, a piece of 'bad press' can become a long-term or fixed problem: and it is certainly a big problem if it's one of the few things that the world knows about a particular country. Media themes and consequently public opinion can occasionally whip each other up into a frenzy on certain topics – such as, for example, whale or seal hunting – and this kind of 'bad press' takes on a life of its own, becoming for as long as it lasts almost as strong as the country's image; certainly capable of 'bringing down' a country's good name altogether if it persists for long enough and generates enough of a storm.

In such cases, public opinion isn't usually very interested in nuances or exceptions or complex debates – and, as I mentioned in the case of Israel in Chapter 6, there are two things which countries need to understand they can never do: one is to have an argument with public opinion; the other is to change the subject.

What countries and their governments often don't seem to appreciate is that public opinion, when it's as strong and widespread as this, is a force of nature, like a hurricane or a volcano, and imagining that you can control it, argue with it, predict its behaviour or even fully understand it, is a dangerous delusion. If your village is built on the slopes of a volcano, and lava starts to flow from the crater, what do you do? Some people, of course, will waste precious time complaining about how unfair it is, and how their village has been standing there for generations, and how they have a perfect right to remain where they are. And of course they are absolutely, 100% correct, just as surely as they are absolutely, 100% doomed.

Others will start moving their possessions somewhere a little safer. No prizes for guessing whether pride or common sense saves more lives.

It is worth remembering that negative publicity in the global media works a lot like scandal in society, and as the English novelist Wilkie Collins observed in his 1866 novel, *Armadale*:

> *...the influence exercised by the voice of public scandal is a force which acts in opposition to the ordinary law of mechanics. It is strongest, not by concentration, but by distribution. To the primary sound we may shut our ears; but the reverberation of it in echoes is irresistible.*

There isn't much that a country can do once it is tainted by such a story in the international media, beyond the basic 'housekeeping' of good damage limitation and efficient media relations to ensure that as much truth as possible gets out, and dignified and timely rebuttals are issued against the more egregious rumours or untruths.

Prevention is much more possible than cure, and the best and only prevention for such episodes (aside from ensuring that the bad things which cause the bad story don't happen in the first place) is working to create the biggest, richest, widest and most complex international image as possible for the country, through every available channel of public and private diplomacy, educational and cultural exchanges, foreign investment and export promotion, foreign aid, tourism, sport and politics. The bigger, richer and more complex a country's image becomes, the better people feel that they know it and its people and institutions, the more resilient it becomes against negative news. The aim, in short, has to be for a country to become far more than a brand.

The most striking example of this fact is surely the United States, a country whose image repeatedly *doesn't* collapse in the face of quite extraordinary international opprobrium, a country which sometimes seems almost to be *trying* to destroy its good name, but never really gets anywhere near succeeding. The reason is that whatever negative stories may emerge in the media about its foreign policy, its economy, its popular culture, its society, its values, its people or its products, such stories are never more than a fraction of the size or weight of the total national story that people hold in their imaginations. The ship is too big to be easily sunk, even by a fairly big hole in its hull (although they did say that about the *Titanic*).

Countries which, on the other hand, are really only known for two or three things will of course find that one bad thing will then constitute a third or a quarter of their entire reputation, and will very likely sink the ship.

I mentioned before that once a negative story starts running, it's impossible to change the subject: but that doesn't mean that countries shouldn't *try* to change the subject. On the contrary, they must try exactly as if they believe that they will succeed in changing the subject, even though it's most likely that they will fail. Engaging on many fronts in every possible form of exchange with people in other countries, carrying on new 'conversations' on every possible topic *including* the controversial topic at the heart of the problem, but never *dominated* by that topic, is not only prevention against the next episode, but may also help to shorten the life of the current episode.

Sooner or later, the story will die, and then the task of enriching the country's reputation must continue in earnest, with clear goals, widespread participation across the private and public sectors, substantial investment and even greater energy.

The question of deserved reputation

But before we even start to think about why the media deals with a country in a particular way, it's worth asking whether that infuriating picture they always paint of the country is actually justified. It is remarkable how frequently governments avoid this question.

I am often contacted by the governments of countries who announce that – apparently – they have an appalling image, and could I do something to fix it? I always answer with another question: 'Might this be because you are an appalling country?'

The governments in question are often rather unhappy with this response, but of course it has to be the first question one asks. In the majority of cases, the problem is a weak image rather than a negative image, and the ambition of many countries today can be characterized as wishing to move out of the margins and into the mainstream of global opinion.

In addressing this challenge, it's always worth asking why the country isn't *already* in the mainstream – or, to put it brutally 'if you're so wonderful, how come you aren't famous?' – since if it proves possible to alter some of these conditions, the country might then start to achieve the kind of recognition which it believes it deserves.

The harsh reality is that, barring their close neighbours, most people in the world really only respect, occasionally think about, claim to know about and generally admire a maximum of 14 or 15 countries apart from their own, and these are all major, industrialized democracies in Western Europe and the English-speaking world, plus Japan and Brazil. This core of admired countries, if you like, forms the exclusive 'downtown area' of Planet Earth.

Most of the other countries that are well known aren't much admired: they are famous because they are trouble-spots (there are usually about another 15 of these at any given moment, such as Iraq, Zimbabwe and North Korea), or because they once enjoyed a high profile, which people who don't know much about them feel they no longer deserve (like Greece, Turkey or Egypt), or because they are indisputably very important but not universally loved, trusted or admired (like Russia, China, America or India). These countries are the planet's 'ghetto' – everyone knows where it is, but only so that they can avoid it.

The remaining 160 countries on the planet largely mind their own business and are consequently ignored by everyone who isn't actively planning to emigrate or go on holiday there. In planetary terms, they're out in the suburbs.

There are six very common reasons for the persistent obscurity of these countries:

1. **They really are marginal.**
The majority of the 160 lesser-known countries have a chronic shortage of what marketers call 'consumer touch-points': people simply don't get many chances to come into contact with them, their products, their culture or their populations.

In some cases this is because the country hasn't been an independent state for very long; in many cases it is because its population or economy are small; only a few of them are well-endowed tourist destinations; almost none of them have had significant possessions or interests abroad; very few of them trade significantly 'above the line' with other countries – in other words, their trading habits are largely industrial, business-to-business or in raw materials or unfinished goods. Such transactions are well below the radar of most ordinary people and the media.

Most of the 160 never feature in most other countries' history books because they have never produced a world-class statesman or stateswoman; their role in history is usually of merely regional significance, their historical moments taking place against a backdrop of 'big history' going on elsewhere; their cultural output is seldom of truly world-class quality *and* quantity. Most of them even lack the picturesque assets of monarchy and aristocracy – the mark of a just state, perhaps, but undoubtedly a loss to their tourist industry.

2.   **They produce few really famous people.**
The other common characteristic of the 160 lesser-known countries is that they have never produced more than a tiny handful of really world-famous individuals, or a really influential and visible diaspora; most of them, in short, have a shortage of popular ambassadors. The Nation Brands Index suggests that people cannot readily picture the inhabitants of more than those 30 admired or notorious countries, and a population without an image is an overwhelming obstacle to the creation of a powerful and positive *national* image.

It is almost a cliché of media theory that 'the media prefers a human interest story': this is simply a reflection of public taste. People are most interested in other people, and one of the big mistakes that countries often make in trying to build their images is that they constantly present inanimate achievements to the world – projects, buildings, historical events, companies, products and services, achievements, statistics, landscapes, policies – everything, in fact, apart from the one thing that people really like to hear about: other people.

And, unfortunately, it's as much about quantity as quality. No country acquires a lasting worldwide reputation for music with one world-class composer or a couple of No.1 hits, nor a reputation for architecture from one world-class architect, nor a reputation for statesmanship from one prominent president, nor, indeed, a reputation for technology from one world-class brand.

As I have often remarked, building a national reputation is like filling a bathtub without a plug, and a country can produce a truly towering international figure but soon fade from the world's memory if he or she is not quickly succeeded by another remarkable figure from the same nation.

3. **They are cursed as well as blessed by their humility.**
It's remarkable how many populations suffer from what I call 'Groucho Marx Syndrome'. The comedian Groucho Marx famously observed that he would never want to join a club that would accept somebody like him as a member, and this appears to be a common characteristic of the human species: some kind of culturally-rooted modesty, a fixation of ineligibility, which prevents all but a very few nations from really shouting about their talents and achievements.

The Americans are naturally inclined to do it, and so are the Swedes and the British and the French, but the majority of other societies have a habit of pulling down people who do too well. Many of them even have special names or proverbs to describe this habit, which they are convinced is unique to their population: the Japanese say that 'the nail which sticks out gets hammered down'; the Australians talk about the 'tall poppies' getting cut down; the 'Law of Jante' is talked about throughout Scandinavia; South Americans refer to the 'chaquetero' – the person who pulls you down by your coat tails – and so it goes on.

I always think it's rather nice to discover that the majority of people in the world are modest, and perhaps it also explains why less than 15% of the world's countries are famous, despite the fact that almost all of them are wonderful.

4.   Most are low-profile countries in high-profile regions.

Whilst the majority of countries remain largely anonymous, people have quite strong ideas and prejudices about most regions and continents: Latin America, South-East Asia, the Middle East, Sub-Saharan Africa, the Mediterranean, the Balkans, Scandinavia, Eastern Europe, 'Old' Europe, Central Asia and so forth.

Many countries are minor players in regions with powerful cultural and geographical identities, and thus have a tendency to be overshadowed by the more powerful and prominent nations within their region, or by the region itself. In most cases, this 'regional image effect' does not work to their advantage. I have written extensively about how the negative continental 'brand' of Africa is vigorously promoted by the aid industry and celebrities like Bono and Bob Geldof, to the great detriment of individual countries within Africa, which find it extremely hard to emerge from this hugely potent image of permanent catastrophe.

5.   They have never done anything about it.

Most countries have never addressed these issues of national reputation in any systematic way, and there is usually a notable lack of joined-up behaviour between the ways in which the different sectors, public and private, do their planning, spending, innovating, marketing and messaging. (Developing logos and slogans and running expensive 'nation branding' spots on international TV do not qualify as 'doing something about it').

There is usually no explicit national consensus on the 'mission', 'vision' and 'style' of the country: if such notions exist, they tend to be very much an unwritten constitution.

Most of the 160 countries possess few mechanisms for aligning the different sectors of their economy or society, few forums for productive and harmonious cross-fertilization between them, and no single body with the responsibility for providing a national steer on reputational issues.

In most cases, there is much that could be achieved by tighter, more frequent and better organized collaboration between foreign policy, domestic policy, culture and the arts, sport, the private sector and especially exports, education, tourism, investment promotion, the financial sector, energy and the media.

6.   **They are boring.**

A high proportion of these 160 countries are moderately stable, moderately peaceful, moderately unexciting places which have done nothing really extraordinary in living memory to render themselves either admired or disgraced. They have succeeded in establishing almost no relevance to people in other countries; there is simply no reason why most people should grant them any of their precious attention.

Most of the 160 suffer from none of the headline-grabbing flaws or catastrophic troubles which might excite major international pity or sympathy; they rarely stick their noses into other countries' business (or, at most, only into their neighbours' business); in politics, most of them are either modest but invisible international team players or don't feature at all in international circles.

Of course, in reality, a great many of them have a truly fascinating history, culture, society, language, traditions and landscape – but in the end, these assets are seldom of a sort to excite more than momentary envy, admiration or curiosity amongst other populations, who are usually far more interested in what goes on at home.

And it *is* possible for one of the 160 invisible countries, once in a while, to emerge into the sunny uplands of the 30 visible countries: but it is a task that cannot be overestimated. It is probably the most difficult thing that a country can ever do.

Picking your battles

The world's media can be divided into two types: the vast majority whose aim, or habit, is to reflect people's existing views, and the tiny minority whose aim, or habit, is to challenge these. Clearly any country that is trying to emerge from the 'anonymous 160' into the mainstream should focus its media strategy on the latter type – although, it should be emphasized, a mere media strategy can't possibly achieve this titanic task on its own.

There is an interesting circular relationship between the media and the 'brand images' of places. In one sense, those images are created or at least amplified and perpetuated by the media, but in another sense they create the media. Take a look at how almost any story featuring more than one place is treated in the media, and it becomes clear that the main elements in the story are the *idées reçues* or stereotypes about those places: much international journalism is simply a process of rehearsing, playing with, sometimes examining and very occasionally challenging those national brand images. A lot of journalism is basically a matter of endlessly redeploying such clichés.

When a country has a clear, simple, well-defined national stereotype, the media will be more comfortable covering that country, and this means that it will feature more regularly in the media, even if the basic journalistic formula is often little more than measuring up the stereotype against the news event and seeing how closely they fit. Countries without strong images may find that they get less coverage generally, because a good story needs strong characters, and a weakly defined nation will often be left out.

This is part of the reason why Mexico, for example, gets more coverage in the international media than Chile, even though just as many good and interesting things go on in Chile. The fact is that Mexico has a very clearly defined 'brand image' which makes an easy and resonant instrument for a journalist to play on. Chile, without a strong image, is a trickier and less noisy instrument to play; and many foreign journalists will pass over the challenge.

At the start of this chapter I observed that some companies are more interested in finding ways of making people buy their product than in developing a product that more people might want to buy. It's important that governments, in the effort to enhance their international standing, don't fall into the same trap as these companies, and end up focusing on the medium rather than the message. Too much so-called 'nation branding' is really only public relations – the attempt to persuade the media to cover your country as positively and frequently as possible.

Good countries, like good companies, should be product-obsessed, not story-obsessed: the media is simply the carrier, not the focus of one's efforts to earn a better reputation. This is absolutely a matter of integrity, and integrity is all: countries that 'play to the gallery' are soon found out, and public opinion is sensitive to attention-seekers, and generally quite adept at distinguishing them from the places with real integrity, a real sense of purpose and a real sense of identity.

The good news is that journalists are, always and forever, short of good content, and will act as a highly effective (and highly cost-effective) conduit for reputation if only one can provide them with the quantity, consistent quality and professionalism that they require. The fate of the media is as much our responsibility as theirs.

The media isn't, of course, the only means by which national reputations are forged and communicated; direct experience combined with word of mouth is equally significant (when, for example, large numbers of people visit a country as tourists or immigrants or investors or students, and pass on their impressions to others); products and services, when their country of origin is explicit, can be tremendously powerful vectors of national standing (consider how the images of Japan and Germany developed between the end of the Second World War and today, largely through the effect of the consumer brands they exported around the world); diplomacy, trade negotiations, international development assistance and the other official channels through which elites communicate can be a critical factor in shaping perceptions of countries; famous people, acts of war, acts of charity, education, history, films, books, works of art, pictures, sporting and cultural events all play their part.

But it is remarkable how many of these phenomena ultimately reach the world's attention through the editorial content of newspapers, magazines, television and the internet. If one doesn't understand how that vector operates, then one cannot begin to think about influencing the image of place.

CHAPTER 11

'Is This About Me?' – The Critical Issue of Relevance

Attempting to influence the image of a place is partly a matter of picking and planning one's battles very carefully. Pitting the puny resources that governments can generally bring to bear against immovable objects (such as trying to contradict or erase long-standing negative perceptions that are deeply rooted in the cultures of other countries) is foolish and can be counterproductive.

After considering the factors described in the previous chapter, such as analyzing why the country isn't already famous, considering to what extent it deserves the reputation it has, and having carefully measured up people's perceptions against the objective reality, it is a good idea to think about which aspects of the country's image are more likely to be subject to influence than others.

Fundamental to this approach is a point which I raised in *Competitive Identity:* the fact that national image is a phenomenon that exists outside the sphere of influence of the country in question. The *identity* of a country exists inside the country and its population, and although it isn't readily amenable to any kind of direct manipulation, it is at least within the country's own sphere of influence. The *image* of a country, however, is in most cases even harder to affect: it is even more complex, even more fragmented, rooted in even more different cultural traditions and even more resistant to deliberate attempts to alteration as national identity; and in addition to all this, it's *not located in the country itself.* It exists, in an incalculably distributed form, in the minds of many millions of different people scattered around the globe.

This is why picking one's battles is so necessary. As a starting-point, it's worth thinking along the following lines:

- Observe *the things that are already moving*: for example, public opinion on climate change, the global economic situation or capitalism in general, and attempt to establish relevance to these issues. In order to *count*, countries must be seen to participate in the global conversations about globally important subjects; if a country has no relevance to the issues that are relevant to its 'public' then it will have little relevance for them. Shifting a stable perception (for example, 'African countries are poor') is always going to be much harder than directing a moving perception (for example, 'African economies may be less vulnerable to the effects of global recession').
- Identify influential target audiences that are actively searching for something, and see if this coincides with something the country has to offer. This isn't rocket science: in fact it's basic marketing, but it's remarkable how many governments devise their 'branding' strategies purely on the basis of what they have to offer, without considering what the people they are targeting actually want.
- Start by focusing on the countries that are naturally downhill of one's own in the global pecking-order. Most people in most countries have pretty strong instincts about which countries are above their own in the hierarchy of nations, and which are below; they tend to respect the ones above, and despise the ones below. Targeting people in downhill countries provides a significantly better return on investment, and is a good technique for building critical mass prior to tackling the more ambitious countries higher up in the hierarchy.
- Identify the beliefs that are *inherently unstable* – perhaps because they are genuinely easy to disprove – or perhaps because their relevance is beginning to decline or be eclipsed by something else. For example, several of the newer member states of the European Union are still widely perceived as having values, standards or conditions which are incompatible with EU membership; so in theory, simply establishing the fact of their EU membership

ought to undermine the prejudice. However, one must be rigorous and objective about this: public opinion often remains strongly attached to negative perceptions about countries, just because they are deeply rooted and picturesque, and will resist even quite categorical proof against such views. As I have pointed out before, people will never voluntarily 'trade down' from an exciting and negative but incorrect perception to a boring and positive but correct one.

• Distinguish between the negative beliefs that exist because, ultimately, people enjoy them and want to believe in them (such as the vampire-infested B-movie image of Romania, which is quite at odds with the modern reality of the place and yet which public opinion in Western Europe is reluctant to abandon), and the negative beliefs which people might be quite relieved to drop but have been prevented from doing so for other reasons (this, as I argue in *Brand America*, is the case with much anti-Americanism – my research suggests that many people feel more comfortable admiring America, and are now relieved to have an opportunity to reassess the country and its influence).

As I explained in the previous chapter, it is normal for people to feel that most other countries have little impact on, or relevance to, their own lives. What limited awareness and knowledge most of us do possess about other countries therefore tends to be quite abstract, and perhaps partly as a consequence of this, rarely changes. These are beliefs rather than opinions, more a series of passive mental images than a constantly-revised or constantly assessed set of active thoughts; the images of other countries form the background to our world view rather than being objects of direct observation or conscious appraisal.

Consequently, even when we hear something new and surprising about another country, this may not affect our mental image of the country at all, which remains securely stowed in the compartment marked 'fundamental beliefs'.

So a country's image can only change if it is *in the correct position to change*: in other words, if it moves from the background to the foreground of our conscious mind. Once relevance is established, the image of a country becomes personally relevant rather than abstract and detached, and change is possible.

The most obvious example of this is when we visit another country as tourists: once we are in a country, it becomes the active focus of our attention, and thus we are fully prepared to change our minds about it. But the shift can also take place at a distance, in other ways: for example, by getting to know somebody from a particular country, experiencing that country's culture or products, reading about it in a book, learning about it in school, or seeing it in a film. These effects are bound to be weaker than first-hand experience of the country, but they can nonetheless bring a country closer to a position of active appraisal within the subject's consciousness.

Still, even when a country is in a position to change its image in people's minds, change will only occur if there is then sufficiently compelling stimulus to do so. This stimulus might be rational or emotional, or it might be a combination of the two: the point is that unless we are 'ready to receive', no stimulus is sufficient; unless people are listening, they won't hear.

The mistake made by most governments attempting to do 'nation branding' is to assume that the key to successful image change lies in the persuasive power of the message which they can present to their target audience. Some believe that as long as the communication is omnipresent and sufficiently attractive and compelling, then surely public opinion will be swayed by the power of emotion. Others take a more rational view, and consider that evidence is more potent than charm: so as long as the relevant facts are presented clearly enough, surely public opinion will bow to the force of reason.

Both are right, and both are wrong: emotion and reason, charm and proof are both indispensable conditions for the changing of opinions, but they are not sufficient, either singly or in combination. Firstly, the audience needs to be prepared to receive and prepared to reconsider. Secondly, there must be a high degree of consistency in both the charm and the proof, and the assault has to be sustained for very much longer than most governments find convenient, before public opinion gradually begins to change.

These two factors are in fact closely linked: the less relevant the country is to the target audience, the more powerful, consistent and sustained the 'stream of evidence and emotion' will need to be in order to change the image. The more relevant the country is to the target, the better the conditions for rapid and profound change in their perceptions of that country.

When we hear something new about another country, everything depends on whether we think 'this is about me' or 'this is about them'. A Mexican citizen, hearing about the US presidential elections on the television, seeing American products in the shops, listening to American music or reading an American book, may well think 'this is about me', and consequently pay close attention: the object is in the foreground, and has the power to add positive or negative weight to his or her existing image of the United States. However, proportionally, this weight will be quite small, because his or her existing perception of the US is already substantial: consequently, each new piece of information is likely to have a correspondingly smaller influence on the whole.

The same Mexican citizen, hearing about the Indonesian presidential elections, seeing Indonesian products and so forth, is more likely to think 'this is about them', and the new information simply won't 'stick'. However, by the same token, any new information that does manage to 'stick' will be large in relation to the small image she or he has about Indonesia, and will form a more significant proportion of the sum total of his or her beliefs about the country.

The conclusion is a paradoxical one, which underlines the fundamental difficulty of changing people's minds about countries. People who already feel that a country is relevant to their lives are probably more inclined to notice the things that country does or says or makes, but may be less likely to change their minds as a result; whereas people who don't feel a country is relevant are less likely to pay attention, but may be more likely to change their minds.

So what determines this all-important relevance, and can it be artificially induced? The simplest and most obvious form of 'natural' relevance comes from geographical and consequently economic and cultural closeness, as with the Mexican/US example. It can be weaker or stronger depending on the political, economic and cultural ties between neighbours: you know more about your neighbours and are more likely to think that anything they do is, at least partly, 'about me'. For example, the Finns pay quite close attention to what goes on in Sweden because of historical, cultural, economic, commercial and social ties between the countries, and tend to exaggerate the importance and relevance of what goes on there. The Faroese and the Greenlanders do so to an even greater degree with respect to Denmark, as do the Irish to the English, the Taiwanese to the mainland Chinese or the Cypriots to the Greeks: all these effects are compounded by complex ties of existing or historical sovereignty.

Relevance also comes from other historical, linguistic or cultural ties: the citizens of Commonwealth countries, for example, are more alert to the relevance of events in each others' countries than to events in many geographically closer countries that don't have so much shared past. British perceptions of Australia, for example, tend to be more active and 'front of mind' than perceptions of Holland, despite the fact that Sydney is 17,000 kilometers from London while Amsterdam is only 350.

Other such links include those between Spain and Latin America (imperial and linguistic), between Jamaica and Ethiopia (religious), between the Netherlands and Indonesia (imperial), Finland and Argentina (because of a shared love of tango) or Finland and Hungary (because of a tenuous linguistic link), Eritrea and Italy (imperial and linguistic), Cuba and China (ideological), and so forth.

Immigration can also create relevance between countries (some British citizens might have become more interested in Lithuania as a result of encountering many Lithuanian workers in Britain; the number of Indian entrepreneurs in Silicone Valley probably means that Californians are much more active in their view of India than they were 20 years ago).

There are many thousands of such links, and all of them provide natural 'pathways' along which influence can be conveyed more readily than between countries which have no direct relevance to each other. But, as I mentioned earlier, for the same reason that 'starting a conversation' between such pairs of countries is easier, so influencing national reputations might be correspondingly harder, because there is more, longer-standing and therefore more deeply rooted knowledge of each other, and quite possibly more prejudice too.

A country which previously occupied another country might find that getting the public's attention in its previous colony is easier, but persuading that public to change its mind about their motivations and character might be harder. Some of these old prejudices can date back centuries but are no less fresh for that. The difficulties which Britain finds today in winning 'hearts and minds' in Iraq and Afghanistan are compounded to an incalculable degree by vivid recollections of its military and political interventions in the nineteenth century; trust and mistrust between the various nations and peoples of the Balkans stretch back even longer; Osama bin Laden, in his attempts to stir up enmity between Muslims and Christians, frequently refers to the Crusades, the last of which took place more than 700 years ago.

It's an interesting question whether old relevance is likely to be more potent than new relevance, or vice versa. Might favour or prejudice caused by recent events be a more powerful effect because it's fresher in people's minds, and based on personal rather than learned or inherited experience? Or do the passage of time, the endless re-telling and eventual mythologization of ancient hurts and insults, generations of indoctrination and other social effects make old prejudices even more powerful than new ones – a sort of 'compound interest' effect?

Certainly, relevance caused by transient phenomena, especially when it is not deliberately caused by human agency, is likely to be among the weaker of these effects. The case of Mexican swine flu, which I mentioned in Chapter 6, is a typical cause of 'transient relevance': an Indonesian person might have found during April and May of 2009 that references to Mexico or experiences of Mexican people, Mexican products and Mexican politics have had a greater than typical resonance because of the 'front-of mind' awareness of swine flu, but if there is no further stimulus or activity from that quarter, the stronger awareness of Mexico will probably be abandoned quite quickly as it has no further usefulness or relevance to most Indonesians.

It's possible, however, that such events leave some trace in the mind, some deeply subconscious 'scar tissue', perhaps nothing that could easily be put into words and hence difficult to identify in research, but just a vague shadow associated with the name of the country, which might just tip the scales ten years later when the original relevance is long forgotten but the same Indonesian is faced with an equal choice between holidaying in Mexico or holidaying in Peru.

Clearly, the relevance of another country can have a direct or indirect influence over the opinions and choices of foreign audiences. If the relevance of another country stems from an association in a particular sector, then its influence will be greatest on decisions related to that sector. If our Indonesian person's awareness of Mexico is mainly associated with swine flu, then this will probably have less of an impact on his or her preparedness to buy a Mexican bicycle than it would have on his or her decision to take a Mexican holiday or eat Mexican food. Undoubtedly, a large component of the relevance of Germany to most British people is the fact that the two countries were at war a generation or two ago; but this negative point of relevance appears to have little impact on British consumers' appreciation of German cars and domestic appliances.

Again, these are deep mysteries, and it has yet to be determined to what extent people tend to lump all their associations about countries into one composite belief, which then has the power to affect their actions relating to all aspects of that country, or to what extent it is possible for different components of a country's image to remain isolated from each other in people's minds.

There are certainly many variants in national image, and the fundamental relevance of countries to foreign populations adds a further layer of complexity to the equation. However, it's perfectly possible to sketch out some straightforward rules of thumb which help to clarify which sorts of activity are least likely and most likely to be effective in altering public perceptions of a country, depending on the kind of relevance that exists between the two countries.

A few examples of these rules are as follows:

Least likely to work: using indirect, impersonal communications to change an image created by *multiple,* direct, personal experiences, over a long period, in many areas including the most critical (e.g. security, religion), and sustained by multiple indirect stimuli, rooted in the culture of the audience, and shared by large parts of the audience's community. Thus, for example, a public relations campaign designed to improve the image of Israel, targeted at Palestinians, would be highly unlikely to achieve its objective.

Unlikely to work: using indirect, impersonal communications to change an image that has been created through direct personal experience, but not sustained for generations and not so widely supported by indirect stimuli. Thus, for example, the 'Shared Values' campaign that the US State Department targeted at Muslims in the Middle East.

Likely to work: using positive, direct experience to create an image where there is currently a mixed or weak image created through indirect experience, and where there is a good reason to trust in the quality of the direct experience. Thus, for example, the opening of a branch of the St Petersburg Hermitage in Amsterdam.

Most likely to work: start with a weakly positive image and either positive or weak secondary or referential image factors (for example, a little-known country in a region with a strong, positive image). Establish strong personal relevance through tourism, exports, cultural relations and foreign policy, with powerful network effects built in. Address with a sustained, consistent, long-term campaign of both proof and emotional factors (building on the weak existing primary or secondary associations for the purposes of credibility). Thus, for example, using tourism, exports and cultural relations to enhance the image of the Faroe Islands – a little-known country that is understood to be in Scandinavia, a highly admired region – in Britain.

There is no question that when one's relationship with a country becomes personal, then that country's image gains greatly in power and significance: this is when a country stops being a brand and becomes an item of experienced reality. The classic demonstrations of this are the one-on-one 'informal ambassador' scenario (having a close friend from a particular country is very likely to create a strong personal prejudice in favour of that friend's home country) or tourism (people will often change their minds completely and permanently about a country after they have visited it).

Extending these powerful 'one-on-one' effects to wider audiences is really the holy grail of competitive identity. As I described in Chapter 7, tourism has an important role to play here, because good destination marketing can create networked or 'viral' marketing effects well beyond the people who actually visit the country: they can become highly effective advocates of the country's image and thus extend the reach of the original promotions well beyond the size of audience that most tourist boards can afford to reach directly through conventional media-based advertising.

A similar challenge is faced by cultural relations, which is demonstrably effective at building highly positive and resilient goodwill towards a country, but extending the reach of this effect beyond the unavoidably limited number of individuals that the country's cultural centres can engage with directly is a real challenge. Programmes which focus on 'teaching the teachers', training journalists, offering scholarships and exchanges to promising business and political leaders, and other methods of working via 'influencers' tend to be quite effective in this area.

Warfare is the most obviously effective way of creating a strong personal relevance with large numbers of people, and it doesn't have to be a negative relevance: America's support for the Western Allies during the Second World War is a significant part of the reason why the United States retains so much goodwill in Europe despite the passage of much time and many differences. By the same token, when one country invades its neighbour – or, worse still, commits crimes of war against its neighbour – then the 'negative relevance' is likely to remain potent and unalterable for many generations.

Additionally, there are the rather rare episodes of (perceived) 'cultural war', such as the Danish cartoons which I mention in Chapter 6 and discussed at greater length in *Competitive Identity*. This is the most dramatic example I have ever seen of a country being almost instantly 'rebranded' as a result of a direct personal connection with very large numbers of people – almost with entire populations – in distant countries.

Admittedly, part of the scale of the damage to Denmark's image in several predominantly Muslim countries may have been due to the fact that this image was rather slender to start with: people's knowledge of Denmark in those countries was probably referential rather than personal – they knew and respected the country only because they knew it was in Scandinavia (this supposition is supported by the fact that before the cartoons were published people in these countries typically gave identical scores on all questions in the Nation Brands Index to Denmark and Norway). In consequence, Denmark's image, although positive, was rather simple and lightweight, and so was more seriously compromised than, for example, America's image after its invasion of Iraq.

The fascinating question is whether it might be possible to achieve a similarly rapid, profound and lasting impact on a country's reputation in a positive direction as real war or perceived 'cultural' war does in a negative direction – and without recourse to military activity.

Charity doesn't seem to do it: America, for example, has donated many billions of dollars in aid to poor countries without an enormous amount of evident benefit to its image either in the receiving country or in the international community. Simply giving money is neither picturesque, memorable or remarkable. Giving money – if you can spare it – is one of the easiest things in the world to do. It doesn't demonstrate any particular expertise, ability, energy, competence or imagination. It is a route often chosen by governments precisely because it's so easy and it's believed to be a way of salving the conscience or proving one's values without needing to do anything difficult or complex. It's often just a way of buying virtue. It's like sponsorship in the commercial world: an excuse not to do anything more difficult or controversial, and a fairly cynical way of buying profile or approval.

Political support can be more effective – it was certainly notice-able that one of the few places where the United States enjoyed great popularity, even at the end of the second Bush presidency, was in Albania, purely as a result of US support for Kosovo. But such foreign policy choices cannot really be determined purely or even partly out of a desire to achieve a positive national image in another country, nor should they be; and it is in any case usually impossible to achieve strong popularity in one country without losing it simultaneously in another.

What is the opposite of insulting a nation? What is the opposite of invading a country? Such questions are unanswerable: the simple fact is that anger or offence are stronger emotions than gratitude or delight – or, at any rate, they are more likely to lead directly to strong actions. If a Syrian feels insulted by 'Denmark', then not buying any more Danish butter is a pretty straightforward response: but if he is delighted by something 'Denmark' has done, how can he express his delight? By buying twice as much butter than he actually needs, and making sure it's Danish? Not only does the positive opposite of the belligerent action not really exist, so the positive opposite of the response to that action doesn't really exist either: there isn't even a word in English for the opposite of 'boycott'.

The search for some kind of 'silver bullet' that will achieve an overnight improvement in a country's image is almost certainly futile: experience suggests that what really works is many smaller deeds, carried out in many different sectors over a much longer period, sustained and made consistent by a clear national strategy.

In conclusion, studying *existing* perceptions towards a given country is absolutely fundamental, and has a greater impact on the options and the potential which that country enjoys than almost anything else. Only through painstaking analysis of the myriad and complex cultural lenses through which each country views each other can a realistic strategy be formulated for earning – probably rather gradually – a truer, more positive and more useful image.

In trying to produce a certain perception of one country in the eyes of another, we are never dealing with a blank canvas, on which it is possible to paint at will: this is a canvas that's already painted, which has been hanging in someone else's house for generations, and which they've grown rather attached to. We can't simply barge in to that house and overpaint without regard to what is already there, or take away the picture and replace it with one that we think looks more like us.

But even that makes it sound easier than it is. In the end, this isn't about painting: it's about doing.

CHAPTER 12

Some Conclusions

There are many strong economic and political arguments for the importance of acknowledging, understanding, monitoring and perhaps influencing the images of places: as I summarized the point in *Competitive Identity,* if a country has a good image, everything is easy; if it has a bad or weak image, everything is twice as hard and costs twice as much.

But there is, I believe, a more fundamental reason for the importance of the subject. The identity and image of the places we inhabit are really a seamless extension of the identity and image of ourselves; it is a natural human tendency for people to identify themselves with their city, region or country. Our sense of self isn't bounded by our own bodies: it extends out into family, neighbourhood, district, region, nation, continent, and ultimately to the human race.

And if the last item on that list seems to be stretching a point, just watch one of those Hollywood blockbusters in which the human race is threatened with annihilation by aliens, and observe your emotional response: perhaps only by a willing suspension of disbelief, but at some level, some part of you will be rooting for the earthlings. We are social creatures, team players to our core, and our core finds meaning and identity almost as much in the team as in the player.

This is why people care so much about where they live, and why people will vote in enormous numbers to place their home town on a board game, or to have their architectural or natural heritage acknowledged by the world as world-beating or at least globally significant. It is why people care so much about the results of international talent contests and beauty pageants, football and cricket and ice-hockey and sailing tournaments, why passions run as high for the *rione* represented in the Palio in Siena or the dragon-boat in Hong Kong as for the nation that wins the chance to host the Olympic Games. What we are endlessly rehearsing is the sublimation of personal identity into group identity, and it is as human as anything we do or feel.

This is also why publics care so deeply about how their nations are perceived by publics in other countries: public diplomacy is finally being driven by public demand. Over the past ten years, I've noticed a striking change in the governments that ask for my advice, or rather a change in the reasons they give for wanting to understand and manage their national image and identity more effectively. It all used to be rather specialized, with governments responding to lobbying from their foreign service or their exporters or their tourist industry, urging them to take responsibility for the country's good name and do what they could to raise the national profile.

Today, all of these reasons are still there, but the driving force, the key incentive, is more likely to be public pressure. Somehow, a feeling dawns in the general consciousness that their country isn't appreciated by people in other countries; that they aren't included or aren't perceived to count in the big global conversations about the things that matter; that they are marginal, ignored, unknown, misrepresented, misunderstood. And this really bothers people. It bothers them for practical reasons – very often because they go abroad to get work and find to their surprise that people are prejudiced against them simply because of where they come from. But most of all it bothers them because their group pride is hurt: people want their nation to *count*. They want to feel proud of where they come from.

When I first started working in this area, my first meetings in a new country were often rather private, rather low-key affairs. Now, as often as not, my first assignment is to speak at a big public conference, with an audience of hundreds, and broadcast on national television. And not all of the people at that conference have a professional stake in the country's good name: of course, many of them represent the tourism industry, exporting companies, public institutions, the foreign service, the culture sector and so forth; but many of them are simply members of the public, come to hear what their government is doing to make their country better known around the world. My emphatic warnings that there is no such thing as 'nation branding', that there is very little that any country can do deliberately to raise its profile, that it takes many generations and much hard work and visionary leadership, seems to do very little to dampen the general enthusiasm.

And throughout the project, that pressure doesn't let up, either: the media will often carry regular reports on how the 'branding' of the nation is going. Coping with their disappointment at the end of my intervention, when logos and slogans aren't unveiled, can be quite a challenge, but generally, this public scrutiny is a good thing. It's extremely important that governments are held to account for everything they do to, and for, the good name of their country and its citizens; and it lessens the temptation for governments to make these important, long-term decisions without recourse to full public consultation and participation.

National prestige directly benefits personal prestige; national shame cripples personal progress; personal identity is inextricably bound up with sense of belonging (both where you come from and where you choose to live, if they are different).

The search for a more competitive national identity can ulti-mately benefit a society beyond its functional usefulness as a means for attracting talent, investment, tourists, respect and adding a pre-mium to exported goods and services. By providing a link between personal achievement and national reputation, these projects give populations an additional incentive for exercising their ambition, imagination, entrepreneurial spirit and hard work.

For many people today, the link between personal endeavour and some greater reward is very weak. To prevent society becom-ing selfish, narrowly individualistic and inwardly directed, it is nec-essary for people to feel that their actions and efforts contribute in some way to something more lasting and more disinterested than personal financial rewards.

The exercise of democracy is the one traditional way in which people can, potentially, feel personally connected to a greater good and to the levers of power in society – but such a feeling does not appear overwhelmingly strong amongst many populations at this point in history. It is not within the remit of this book to explore the reasons for this; but it almost certainly has much to do with the sheer size of national populations today. The rewards of democracy are not an absolute value, but exist in proportion to the size of the electorate, and when one citizen's vote accounts only for a millionth part, a ten-millionth part or a billionth part of the final decision, its value becomes merely symbolic, and participation becomes hard to sustain.

If we can introduce a new formula that links personal effort to a wider international recognition for the country then our work is doubly worthwhile.

It used to be a commonplace of state propaganda to speak of people's 'patriotic duty' to work hard and to become more productive for the benefit of society at large. Perhaps this aspect of the competitive identity project is nothing more than a twenty-first century interpretation of the 'patriotic duty', where the rewards are no longer a matter of winning a war or rebuilding a battered economy: today, we speak of a better image and consequently a premium positioning for products, people, culture, services, destinations and ideas. But the link between what people do in their daily work and lives, and the benefits that they accrue as citizens of their country, is equally beyond dispute.

It is my hope that this process can not only build a country's reputation by connecting the genius of its people to the needs of the global marketplace and global society, but also by creating a meaningful link between private enterprise and the common good.

1 The Anholt-GfK Roper Nation Brands Index, launched in 2005, is a regular survey of around 20,000 individuals in 20 countries which measures, analyses and tracks perceptions of 50 countries. The Anholt City Brands Index performs a similar analysis of cities. Further information on the surveys is available at www.simonanholt.com/research.
2 Armando Sapori: *Studi di Storia Economica Medievale,* Florence (1946), quoted in Simon Anholt: *Brand New Justice,* Elsevier (2003).
3 Richard Wilkinson and Kate Pickett: *The Spirit Level,* Allen Lane, London (2009).
4 Daniel Kimmage: *The Al-Qaeda Media Nexus,* Radio Free Europe, Washington, D.C. (2008).
5 Simon Anholt: *Brand New Justice*, Palgrave Macmillan, London (2001).
6 Michel Foucault: *Naissance de la biopolitique: Cours au Collège de France,* Gallimard & Seuil, Paris (1978–1979). The author is indebted to Sienna Smale-Jackson at the University of Otago for pointing out the link between Foucault and place branding.
7 Michel Girard: *States, Diplomacy and Image-Making – What is New?* in Chong and Valencic (Eds): *The Image, the State and International Relations,* LSE, London (1999).
8 Quentin Peel: *An Ideal Image – A Journalist's View* in Chong and Valencic (Eds): *The Image, the State and International Relations,* LSE, London (1999).
9 Egypt, Indonesia, Malaysia and Turkey. We use the term 'Muslim country' as shorthand for countries with predominantly Muslim populations.
10 At the 95% confidence interval.
11 Simon Anholt and Jeremy Hildreth: *Brand America: The Mother of All Brands*, Cyan Books, London, 2003.
12 Cold War U.S. official Paul Nitze (1907–2004) to Gordon Gray, the first director of the Psychological Strategy Board (PSB), established in 1951 by President Truman 'to produce unified planning for American psychological operations'; originally cited in Kenneth Osgood: 'Total Cold War: Eisenhower's Secret Propaganda Battle at Home and

Abroad' (Lawrence, Kansas: University of Kansas Press, 2006), p. 43, p. 45; appeared in Public Diplomacy Press and Blog Review for October 19–20, 2006.

13 Robert M. Gates: 'Landon Lecture', given at Kansas State University, Manhattan, KS, 26 November 2007, quoted in Daryl Copeland and Evan Potter: *Public Diplomacy in Conflict Zones: Military Information Operations Meet Political Counter-Insurgency* in the *Hague Journal of Diplomacy*, 3 (2008) 277–297.

14 David Steven and Alex Evans: *Towards a theory of influence for twenty-first-century foreign policy* in *Engagement: Public Diplomacy in a Globalised World,* Foreign and Commonwealth Office, London (2008).

15 Daryl Copeland: *Guerrilla Diplomacy: Rethinking International Relations,* Lynn Rienner, Boulder, Colorado (2009).

16 A skunkworks is a group of people who, in order to achieve unusual results, work on a project in a way that is outside the usual rules. A skunkworks is often a small team that assumes or is given responsibility for developing something in a short time with minimal management constraints. Typically, a skunkworks has a small number of members in order to reduce communications overhead. A skunkworks is sometimes used to spearhead a product design that thereafter will be developed according to the usual process. The name is taken from the moonshine factory in Al Capp's cartoon, 'Lil' Abner.'

17 According to the Pew Research Centre's State of the News Media Report for 2009, newspaper advertising revenues have declined by 23% over the last two years. While the recession has made matters much worse, the evidence suggests that this is a long-term tendency that points to terminal decline unless the industry can reinvent itself. Source: CP Chadrashekhar: *Fading Print*, Frontline, Volume 26 – Issue 12, Jun. 06–19, 2009.